SURFING THE ASIAN WAVE

SURFING
THE
ASIAN WAVE

How to survive
and thrive in the
new global reality

Steve McGinnes

Marshall Cavendish
Business

Published in 2020 by Marshall Cavendish Business
An imprint of Marshall Cavendish International

A member of the
Times Publishing Group

Other Marshall Cavendish Offices:
Marshall Cavendish Corporation, 99 White Plains Road, Tarrytown NY 10591-9001, USA • Marshall Cavendish International (Thailand) Co Ltd, 253 Asoke, 12th Floor, Sukhumvit 21 Road, Klongtoey Nua, Wattana, Bangkok 10110, Thailand • Marshall Cavendish (Malaysia) Sdn Bhd, Times Subang, Lot 46, Subang Hi-Tech Industrial Park, Batu Tiga, 40000 Shah Alam, Selangor Darul Ehsan, Malaysia.

Marshall Cavendish is a registered trademark of Times Publishing Limited

National Library Board, Singapore Cataloguing in Publication Data

Name(s): McGinnes, Steve.
Title: Surfing the Asian Wave : How to survive and thrive in the new global reality / Steve McGinnes.
Description: Singapore : Marshall Cavendish Business, 2020.
Identifier(s): OCN 1124641054 | ISBN 978-981-4868-46-4 (paperback)
Subject(s): LCSH: Corporate culture—Asia. | Business etiquette—Asia. | Success in business—Asia.
Classification: DDC 650.1095—dc23

Printed in Singapore

For John,
who always wanted me to see the things
that he never got the chance to.
I love and miss you.

"And the end of the fight is tombstone white
with the name of the late deceased,
and the epitaph drear: A fool lies here
who tried to hustle the East."
— Rudyard Kipling

Contents

Introduction

"Just before a tidal wave hits, the tide gets pulled way out. The water just disappears.

I read about a young girl standing on a beach just before a tsunami. She watched the water disappear and she knew what it meant. She wasn't an expert, but she had learnt a little about tidal waves at school.

Whilst other people on the beach just watched, she guided her family and friends to higher ground. Having just enough relevant, actionable information, at the right time – that's what counts."

— Dane, consultancy director, 20-year Asia veteran

Our biggest challenges and greatest opportunities are global.

The climate catastrophe that will impact us all, a potential economic collapse that will destroy businesses and erase the savings of millions, the rise of political and religious extremism – all these are global problems that can only be solved by cross-border, cross-country and cross-cultural solutions.

The better we understand each other, the more likely we are to find solutions together to prevent these catastrophes.

At the same time, our greatest chances for success, reward and growth as countries, businesses and individuals are also global. Opportunities now lie beyond national borders and cultures. Your future success will be global.

But we can't succeed at what we don't understand.

This is not an academic study, travel guide or traditional business book. It is a book that addresses and prepares you for one of the single biggest changes in human history. A change that if you ride it, could lift you to the top of your chosen field, or ignored will rush right over the top of you and leave you gasping for air.

The world-changing collision of Asia and the West is happening. Understanding how to navigate, act and lead in the new converged world will become the most valuable, sought-after and useful skill that any 21st-century professional can possess.

How have we got here? Technology has brought humanity together, yet simultaneously isolates us as individuals. Each of us has a public social media voice through which we can speak to millions, whilst the world's mass media is tightly controlled, promoting the agenda of a handful of moguls who operate far beyond national borders. The global population continues to grow worryingly, and huge demographic shifts put pressure on governments to support those too young or too old to work. We subject the planet to unprecedented abuse, whilst simultaneously spending more than ever on our own personal health and well-being.

Yet underneath it all, like two giant tectonic plates, the West and Asia are crashing together. As the ground buckles beneath us, all of the activity, progress, fear and hope on the surface will be impacted. Mountains will shake, buildings will fall and tidal waves will hit the coastlines of our cultural and economic islands.

These are unprecedented shifts, and we simply cannot predict exactly what is going to happen. But we can be prepared for it.

Business leaders are trying to stay ahead of the waves. The Economist Intelligence Unit reported that the majority of the CEOs they questioned were now looking to emerging markets for their new customers. Some 71% of them intended to have more people on the ground in new countries, and in the next three years, 78% intended to have more cross-cultural teams.

The biggest blocker to their future success? They believed it was cross-cultural misunderstandings.

"The real challenge is the unknown unknowns. Things that we are so ignorant about that we don't know they are things we are ignorant about. If we know that we don't know something, we can at least try to find out about it. If we don't know that we don't know, well, then we are simply lost."
— Simon, finance director, 15 years in Asia

As with any large sociological, cultural or economic shift, there are pockets of resistance, pushback and challenge.

Seen up-close, these counter-movements may seem as though they are themselves major forces for change, e.g. the government initiatives, legislation and popular movements that are in opposition to globalisation, pushing back on the mass movements of people and the economic interdependency of East and West. China and the US's trade tariff bickering, politicians taking a populist anti-immigration stance and anti-globalisation protesters all make a lot of noise, for a while, but slowly and quietly things continue on the same path of convergence as before.

"Despite his advisers telling him otherwise, Canute was unable to hold back the tide. Neither will those opposing economic globalisation be able to hold back what is the tide of the times. There are people who hope to break the interdependence of the world's economies. And some even advocate decoupling the world's two largest economies. Such intentions, which have become evident since the trade frictions escalated between China and the United States, are trying to halt the momentum of economic globalisation. But history will ultimately prove them foolish."

— Zhou Shuchun, Editor-in-Chief, *China Daily*

On the other side of the convergence, the American journalist George Packer once wrote that rejecting globalisation is "like rejecting the sunrise". You can dispute it as much as you want, but it is going to happen anyway.

This book's division of the world across a single axis is too basic, binary and oppositional for many people's tastes. It is true that the world is much more complex and nuanced than this. But I would respond that the perfectly nuanced, detailed, deep, robust and unarguably definitive study doesn't exist, and if it did, it would be too big to read and too detailed to apply in the real world.

This book is built on the insights and experience of real people, leaders in their fields, who have often learnt the hard way, and are happy to pass on that learning, so you don't have to learn the hard way too. The key points they make are further developed with the support of solid academic findings from respected sources, and sometimes my own humble thoughts and insights. Each chapter contains a list of suggestions for how you can use the key points in the real situations you will find yourself in.

Our best hope of surviving and thriving in this new global reality – as individuals, businesses and even nations – is through understanding each other better. At this point in history, the "Other" that the West needs to better understand is Asia.

This is not a one-directional shift – we should not need to prepare for a future in which the West will be consumed or subjugated by Asia. This truly is a convergence. The future will be a combination of both sides. Asia will increasingly feel the influence of the West, and in a similar fashion to us, they will have to understand the West better than they do now in order to succeed.

The impact may feel one-sided because from our perspective we are only seeing the impact that Asia is having on us. But from the other viewpoint, our impact on Asia is just as dramatic and requires a similarly steep learning curve.

Both sides are going through this together – another thing we have in common. Asia and the West trade more, invest more, share more, interact more and are more mutually reliant on each other than ever before in history. I believe this is the result of the sheer momentum that the tectonic plates have built up, and what we are seeing is cultures and economies getting pushed into each other, and previously separate worlds becoming jumbled together.

But momentum can only take us so far. Imagine for a moment how much more effective our interactions could be if we understood each other better. Think of the results we could deliver together in innovation, information technology or healthcare if we removed some of the barriers to communication, and developed a much better understanding of how each side thinks.

Could we work together to develop solutions to the world's ecological problems if we better appreciated each other's deepest motivations and ways of seeing the world?

What greatness could we achieve, and how rewarding would that be, if we improved our understanding of each other by even just a fraction?

But we don't really have a choice. The tidal wave is coming, whether we understand what's on the other side or not.

What we need is just enough relevant, actionable information, at the right time. As the girl on the beach knew, that can make all the difference.

"I worked with a Texas billionaire. He had been successful in the US and in Europe, so he decided it was time to expand into Asia. 'If it works here, it will work there' was his mantra.

But relationships stalled, things took longer, they couldn't get access to the right people, promising conversations went nowhere and the right decisions weren't forthcoming.

After spending millions on the Asia push, they had to shut it down and walk away. It hadn't worked because they didn't – or wouldn't – understand that things are simply different here."

— Jay, Chief Data and AI Officer and serial entrepreneur

Tools, Terms & Tips

This book is divided into 11 subject chapters. The chapters can be read sequentially, or you can work through them in any order that suits you, and you don't need to have read a preceding chapter to fully understand the next one.

It makes sense to read the Introduction and this chapter first, but from now on, if you want to head straight to a particular chapter, that's your choice. This should make it simple to get information on a topic of special interest or relevance to you – or to refresh your memory on a subject.

Our conceptual axis

The anthropologist Edward Hall, in his book, *The Silent Language*, identifies two types of national cultures: "low context" and "high context".

Low-context cultures have greater belief in the importance of individuals and their accomplishments. They create, follow and enforce clear sets of rules, and they believe in, and try to ensure, fairness for everyone. They are highly communicative and try to be open and direct in what they want and what they are saying. They see time as linear, and they believe in cause and effect.

Low-context cultures include Europe, the UK, Australia, New Zealand, South Africa, the USA and Canada. These are countries with a predominantly Northern European heritage, and countries that were heavily influenced by European powers during their colonial periods. They are not neatly placed together geographically, but for ease of recognition we will refer to them in this book as the "West".

High-context cultures, on the other hand, are much more group-orientated (family, team, company, country) and more relationship-led. They are less direct in communication and rely on others knowing what they want to communicate rather than having to be explicit. Rules are seen as flexible, and time is a relative term. Events are not felt to be simple and discrete, but interconnected and holistic.

High-context cultures would include China, Japan, Korea, India, Bangladesh, Pakistan, Thailand, Vietnam, Myanmar and Cambodia. Whilst this is also not an exact geographical or even cultural label, for simplicity we will refer to these countries and cultures in this book as "Asia".

Of course, in some high-context cultures, there will be some low-context people, and vice versa, but overall, Hall felt that all cultures fall somewhere on the axis of low to high context.

Scientists have attempted to unearth the causes of these fundamental differences. They may be rooted in different thinking styles (Socratic principles of self-determinism vs. Confucian principles of harmony), religion (Judeo-Christian vs. Buddhist/Hindu), or even the type of agriculture (seasonal grain harvests requiring the organising of many people for short periods of time vs. rice farming requiring diligence all year round).

This book recognises that the differences do exist, even whilst disagreement on the root cause remains. The world contains two very different viewpoints and because of new technology, global commerce, international brands and ease of travel, these high-context and low-context cultures are more likely than ever to come face-to-face with each other on a regular basis.

Use your discretion

Often in this book concepts or behaviours are positioned in a simple opposition, with ways of thinking or behaving presented as being on two ends of an axis. For example: the importance of the individual in the West versus the primacy of the group in Asia; Westerners' drive to stand out compared to Asians' need to blend in; the West's desire for equality versus the Asian preference for hierarchy.

These positional statements are true – insofar as they are true enough to be useful. They are demonstrated by empirical evidence and brought to life through first-hand anecdotes. But be aware, we are painting with a broad brush.

Some Japanese men are taller than some Dutch men, but we can still make the statement, "The Dutch are taller than the Japanese", without huge fear of contradiction. But we need to also acknowledge that you may likely meet some very tall Japanese men.

Some Asian people are more individualistic than some Westerners, and some Westerners are more averse to the spotlight than some Asians. Some large Western companies are more hierarchical than many Asian startups, but the exceptions do not disprove the general principles we are making.

I have drawn on examples from working with businesses in Asia, but there is no one single type of business. Some companies remain true to the fundamentals I outline, whilst others have adopted a much more Western style and set of (visible) values, which is seen in attitudes toward hierarchy, timekeeping, corruption, etc.

As with individuals, treat each company as unique, whilst considering the overarching points made.

So, when reading this book, place the ideas on the conceptual West-versus-Asia axis, but remind yourself that reality happens somewhere in from the extreme edges.

And remember that a country's culture is not confined to its geographical space. Sure, if you are in Tokyo, then you are clearly in a high-context, relationship-led, hierarchical Asian culture. But you can also find this high-context culture "exported" to your territory.

For example, say your packing facility is in negotiation with a Japanese investment bank, and your meeting room is full of Japanese representatives of that company. You may physically be in Ohio, but if you want that meeting and the relationship to go well, then you need to be aware of the behaviours, protocols, thought processes, hierarchies and relationship biases that will be present. For the duration of those meetings, you would be wise to treat that meeting room as though it was on Japanese soil and take the learnings in the book and apply them as directly as if you were in Tokyo.

If your automobile production plant has been bought by an Indian conglomerate, then when you are talking, working, negotiating with your new Indian bosses and colleagues, you need to mentally be in Asia. You may be sitting in your office in England, but in cultural terms, during those interactions, you should think and act as though you are in Bangalore.

If you are giving a Chinese delegation a tour of your gold mine, the fact that you are 100 feet under northern Australia is irrelevant – mentally you need to be deep inside China.

Watch for the Dunning-Kruger effect

The Dunning-Kruger effect is a term for the cognitive bias that allows people who don't know much about a topic to believe they are experts in it.

The term derives from David Dunning and Justin Kruger's original study in 1999, "Unskilled and Unaware of It: How Difficulties in Recognising One's Own Incompetence Lead to Inflated Self-Assessments".

In the study, they analysed the behaviours and beliefs of a bank robber, McArthur Wheeler, who robbed banks unmasked, but with his face covered in lemon juice. Having read that lemon juice could be used as invisible ink, he mistakenly believed that putting it on his face would make him invisible to the security cameras. (This is all 100% true.)

Presumably he had seen the words "lemon juice" and "invisible" together somewhere and with no other knowledge or expertise came to a set of false conclusions. The little bit of information he had gave him a hugely inflated belief in his understanding and allowed him to make giant, dangerous assumptions, which he then acted on.

The less someone knows about a subject, often the more confident they are about it, as they are not aware of the complexity, history and nuances of the subject. If they were more aware, ironically they would not be so confident.

You may see "Aha! Dunning-Kruger!" moments in a number of our stories in the book. Our contributors overcame the effect and prospered to tell the tale, but at the time they were as susceptible to it as anyone else.

The Dunning-Kruger effect is probably at the root of many of the best-known, and less well-known, West/Asia business and cultural failures. Keep your Dunning-Kruger radar turned on as you read this book – and out in the world.

1:
Relationships

"Without humility and an effort to understand, you can't build a relationship of trust. Without a relationship of trust, you can't do business."
— Ian McLernon, President and CEO of Rémy Cointreau Americas, 7 years spent in Asia

"In Asia, it is likely you will break the rules at the start. Did you sit in the right chair? Did you give the right greeting? Did you present your card the correct way? If you are arrogant or unthinking in your attitude or approach, then this will be seen as indicative of your character. Then it is likely that you will never be able to successfully do business with those people."

Ian is solidly built, incredibly focused and immaculately dressed. We meet for lunch at a restaurant on a pier in Singapore. Sitting with him makes me feel like I got dressed in the dark. The soft Irish accent, the well-cut suit, the watch, the haircut, the smile, all combine to give an impression of elegant, conservative authority.

Ian works with luxury brands, and luxury is all about understanding the impression you are conveying and paying attention to the details.

"If you are humble and try to understand, if you start the relationship off in the right way, if you show interest in getting things right, then, even if you make a misstep, it will likely be overlooked."

As we eat, Ian becomes more animated. He gestures with one hand whilst holding a fork in the other. He talks passionately about his years in Asia.

"A trusting relationship is not a short-term thing. You can start to build it from the first meeting, but you won't actually have it for many years. That is where many expats, with their three-year contracts, go wrong. You can't build trust in such a short time.

If you are lucky, your predecessor, your company or your brand has established some trust and you can build on that."

Each country is different and has its own rules. There are common Asian foundations across China, Japan, Korea, South-east Asia, but they vary across specific aspects. Within each country, individuals can succeed beyond what we may see as a rigid structure by effectively managing relationships.

To give just one example, in South Korea most of the hugely successful companies are family-owned and run. That aligns with foundational Asian values. However, smart, driven individuals who are not part of the family can still do very well in those companies. But they need to operate within that framework.

They build strong relationships with the key family decision-makers. They follow the protocols of a family business. They display respect and humility. But simultaneously they are able to bring in a fresh perspective and escape some of the family restrictions and expectations. This allows them to work effectively and even to drive the required change gently from within the organisation.

A number of successful and dynamic Asian business leaders grew up in Asia, so they are inherently grounded in an understanding of that culture and its relationship norms, but were then educated or gained professional experience in the West. They bring home alternative ways of thinking, building it into the solid and effective Asian values and principles they know so well.

This can be seen not only in the behaviours and results of successful individuals and companies, but also in how whole cultures and countries are starting to behave.

"Asians are not becoming Westernised! You would be naive to think so. They are selecting and adopting successful Western ideas, ways of thinking and practices, then integrating these into their existing traditions, relationships and ways of working. They are cherry-picking the best bits. That's what's driving the huge Asian success stories.

In the West, we have been really slow to see what is happening. And we still aren't adopting the same principles. The learnings and successes are going one-way."

It is clear that Ian thinks we should be paying a lot more atten-tion to what Asian brands and businesses are doing. Not just to stay ahead, but to learn from them.

"Those who fail in Asia are those that do not appreciate what there is to learn here. They aren't inquisitive. They don't enjoy talking to people. They are not open. They don't build strong relationships. As a result, they will never build respect or gain trust.

Title is important in Asia, but don't forget that how you interact with others is what really demonstrates your position in the hierarchy. How you behave conveys your power, not what is written on your card – these are just words. The relationships and behaviours are what counts."

As we finish lunch and pay the bill, Ian tells me a story that brings to life the importance of trust and relationships.

"I built up a strong relationship with one of our customers. He was the family business patriarch, an older gentleman in his 70s. Our companies had been working together for perhaps three years, and we had met a number of times.

When it was announced that I was leaving, he took the time to bring me into his life. He took me to his church. He took me to his favourite restaurant. Were we friends? Probably not, but perhaps we were starting to be. In the West we try to separate work and life. We think business and friendships are separate. They are not. They are extensions of each other.

In Asia, when the line between business and friendships begins to blur, that is when trust begins."

Many Westerners are surprised at how deep and interconnected the webs of personal, family and business relationships are in Asia.

The family network extends beyond the standard Western nuclear family, to extended family connections and even the much larger clan network and relationships.

Friendships formed in the neighbourhood whilst growing up, at school or in army service are highly valued and nurtured. Childhood friends will see each other at Lunar New Year or other festivals and gatherings. School alumni groups meet regularly, have social media groups and mobile platforms. Army cohorts have regular get-togethers. They act as personal and professional support networks. Advice is sought, business deals done and jobs given, all within the group.

Not only are the groups stronger and larger than in the West, they are not distinct and separate the way Western groups often are. In Asia these groups overlap and interweave. Families work together, army friends employ each other, fathers hire sons-in-law, brothers-in-law help each other, brothers run competing departments, neighbours become colleagues, and colleagues become friends.

In Asia, a person's relationships are the conduit for almost every job opportunity, introduction, promotion or deal they will ever have. These relationships are built on their (or their family's or friends') reputations. The intimate interconnectedness of relationships means that your reputation is widely known, or instantly researchable. Your reputation and your relationships are your most valued assets.

Karsten Warnecke of the Asia-Europe Foundation (who we hear more from in the chapter on Time Perception) illustrates the different emphasis on relationships in Asia, drawing on his experience working with global leaders:

"When the Asia-Europe Meeting (ASEM) was set up, the Asians wanted summits. Big, public gatherings with dinners and events and speeches and ceremony. The Westerners wanted meetings. They saw summits as a waste of time; better to just get together in small groups and agree actions.

That is what many Westerners misunderstand. They don't realise that without the relationship-building, there can be no action.

In the West, we are conditioned to agree actions and business with the other side primarily – and only when the project is under way, then we start to build a relationship with the other side. Action first, relationship second.

In the 'East', it is the other way around. You take time to build the relationship first. Then and only then, with a strong relationship of trust and respect in place, do you start to do business.

Westerners often don't understand that. We got the Westerners to the summit with the promise of bilateral meetings happening around the summit, where the actual work would be done!

You need to show your face, figuratively and literally. Asians will walk into a room and see who is and isn't there. Who took the time to show up. Who showed a commitment. And who didn't. It's noticed and remembered. And not just whether a country is there or not. Who is representing that country is key too.

You have an election happening? You have a crisis? It

doesn't matter. The leader should still be there, if they cherish the relationship. Sending an underling doesn't cut it.

An Asian host country held a commemorative summit. A few countries didn't feel it was worth the head of state going. What would be achieved? It was noticed. When all the representatives arrived, they were ushered into a room for a meeting. The heads of state got plush leather armchairs. The non heads of state, the underlings sent instead of the head, got simple chairs. That's how the host showed their opinion of sending juniors, without having to actually say anything. The countries understood.

In Asia you have to show up. You have to demonstrate your dedication, not just say it; otherwise it's just seen as 'blah blah blah'.

Once you build the relationship, follow the formalities, observe the process and protocols, then you can start to be a little more direct with your requests. With some Chinese I am direct. Others might perceive it as rude, but because I have taken the time to build up that relationship, instead they say I am 'candid'!"

Navneeta and I meet in the offices of a major global media company. Art and awards on the walls. Food and snacks spread out for staff and guests to enjoy. Glass-fronted fridges filled with soft drinks, wines and beers.

Navneeta is small and elegant. In an industry that has its own self-imposed uniform, Navneeta dresses in a manner that whilst wholly professional and appropriate, reflects who she is, not where she is. We take up residency in a small conference room and sip from tall, thin cans of diet Coke.

"From an Asian point of view, a lot of Asians secretly believe Westerners are entitled. That they get given opportunities because of where they are from, not because of talent or hard work.

On the other end of the spectrum, there are also a lot of Asians who still look up to Westerners, who believe they have the answers. They want to ask the Westerners, 'Lead me!'

It's like in postwar Britain when the class system began to erode. People used to looked up to the aristocracy. Then they realised these lords and ladies were just like them, no smarter, just the same. Then they started to hold them in contempt.

My advice: Before you start trying to tell people what to do, work your butt off. Demonstrate why you are in the role. Show that you are there by hard work and talent, not because of the colour of your skin. That way, you build solid relationships across both sides of the table. Both sides respect you."

We stop for a few moments, as Navneeta remembers she needs to instruct someone to organise her ticket for a trip to Japan in a few days. A few taps of the keyboard on her laptop and we continue talking. The topic has shifted to how to engage.

"When you can forget who you are, lose the baggage you brought with you and see from a neutral perspective, then you have crossed the boundary. Then the relationships move from superficial, functional ones to deeper ones. Then, even when you make a mistake, people will forgive it because they intuitively know where it has come from.

Building your local personal relationships is vital. You need people outside of the workplace that you can ask for help and advice. You need people that you feel comfortable saying to them, 'I don't know. Can you help me?' This is vital when you are learning and growing, transitioning between roles or building new contacts."

Research by Ronald Burt (University of Chicago) and Katarzyna Burzynska (Radboud University in the Netherlands) from 2017 looked at the number, type and depth of relationships held by thousands of people, including businessmen and entrepreneurs, in China.

The research showed that those with larger, more open networks were more successful in business than those with smaller, more closed networks.

The research demonstrated that trust was strongest in those relationships where contact was regular. This makes sense in light of what we have heard from our experts. The research also showed that the contact does not need to be formal or face-to-face; any means of engaging is effective for keeping the relationship and the trust strong. Even dormant relationships can be reanimated with a call or a renewed connection, opening up opportunities for job-seeking, business deals or referrals.

Interestingly, a large number of successful relationships (75%) were found to be from "unknown sources" – they were not a schoolmate, family member or military contact, but were a connection made via a connection. This means that fruitful relationships can, and should be, built beyond your immediate circle.

Bob, a global creative director, knows about the positive effect that strong relationships can have. After 20 years living and working in Moscow, Bob is now back home in Australia. But you can tell he is getting itchy feet again. When he talks about Russia he lights up.

Bob looks like the archetypal Aussie. Open personality, infectious smile. Enjoys a beer and a good time. But scratch the surface and Bob is a truly global guy. He met his wife whilst in Moscow. They have a young son.

"Russia isn't a Western country, it is much more Asian in its thinking. Westerners get confused. They think Russians have the same way of thinking as them, because they look the same as them. They don't. Group. Loyalty. Honour. Much more Asian.

Once you make strong connections, people will do any-thing for you. If you asked to borrow $100 from a Russian friend, they would give you their last $50, and then borrow another $50 to give you.

We used to call people fresh in from the West 'peaches'. Soft on the outside but with a hard-to-crack core. As Western-ers, we find it relatively easy to make friends in a short time, but often that friendship can be somewhat superficial.

Russians are more like coconuts, hard on the outside and difficult to have a breakthrough with. But there is so much good stuff hidden inside.

There is an old bit of Russian advice about not smiling around strangers – after all, if you don't know them, why would you smile at them?"

This notion goes deep. It is intrinsic to the understanding of the nature of friendship outside the West.

"It takes more time and effort to make friends, because friend-ship is something that is of very high value. This is rooted in the need for real trust between friends in societies that often have not been able to trust their own institutions or governments. Friends, like family, are the central social support network that people rely on.

I have a personal example in my relationship with a man I hired to drive for me, Max. Over the course of about 12 months, Max and I slowly developed a friendship, a relationship that eventually extended to my whole family. From that point on, Max went far beyond the requirements of being a mere driver.

The perfect example happened on a Sunday morn-ing, which was Max's day off. I suffered a rather horrendous broken leg in an accident and was transported to the hospital emergency room. I was heavily sedated and after a few hours woke to find Max at my bedside. He was busily directing all the nurses and doctors to make sure I was being looked after properly. He stayed with me all afternoon and into the evening, and when it was finally decided to airlift me to France for sur-gery, Max (through a few 'connections' – he was ex-military) arranged for a police escort for my ambulance to the airport, even to the point that the officers were the ones who lifted me onto the jet.

The point is that actual friendship for Russians is a commitment to do absolutely anything for your friends. A com-mitment they take very seriously. I never did found out how Max knew I was in hospital. He wouldn't tell me."

In Asia, compared to the West, there is a lot more informal power in place through relationship influence. This is the "soft power" that lurks in the shadows. It is not overt or obvious – in fact it may have nothing at all to do with the official hierarchy – but it can be equally important.

Joanna, a branding agency CEO who has spent over 20 years working in Asia (we hear more from her in the chapter on Risk & Face), says:

"In Bangkok, the team secretary wielded a huge amount of power. On paper she was the lowest support function, but in reality her knowledge, relationships, influence and connections gave her power. To get a visa sorted or a passport problem dealt with would ordinarily take weeks, but for her it would be done in hours. She had the connections.

When our office was getting too full, we were given some space in the next office tower. We looked for some volunteers to move across to the nicer, newer, better-equipped neighbouring building. It was a no-brainer. Then myself and my boss, the VP, worked out seating plans, etc. But because we hadn't consulted the team secretary about it, she blocked the move. She managed to sabotage, undercut and undermine the whole thing. The global VP had to back down. We never made the move."

This shows that it is always important to share and socialise ideas across the team. Try to engage a wider circle of people than you would think is necessary, who may not be part of the official decision-making process. These people likely won't have any specific comments or suggestions, but they need to know they were asked. Getting their buy-in may be what makes the difference between success and failure.

As a Westerner, you need to actively and consciously do what an Asian may automatically do. Understand the relationships in place, determine the roles they play in the power structure, and stay on the right side of them!

Tobias and I meet at a climbing wall in a mall. It is Saturday morning and the space is just starting to fill up. He is dressed in a cut-off t-shirt, which shows his defined arms and "full sleeve" tattoos. When he sees me, he drops off the wall and we take a seat together to one side of the activity. Tobias works for a big global German company. I suspect he looks more corporate from Monday to Friday.

"Westerners get the impression that Asians aren't loyal. That they are self-serving and will change companies at a moment's notice, for a better deal or a bigger salary. That is true from our perception, but in fact they are just valuing a different set of relationships. Asian relationships are much more personal.

Loyalty is towards a person, or a group of people, such as a family. This is seen in the loyalty that people have for a family business, but not so much for a big, faceless corporation. Western companies often treat people just as assets. So in Asia, people respond accordingly and, you could say, appropriately.

We need to create compelling reasons for loyalty. Be a great place to work that actually values its people. We need to be sincere. You don't achieve that by putting inspirational quotes on the wall, putting down bean bags or buying a new coffee machine! Value people – like friends and family would.

Often when a new senior person comes in, they will bring a whole level of people below them. An instant network of trusted colleagues that they know they can rely on. That they have already built a loyal connection with. Immediate, reliable relationships.

Professional relationships in Asia are deeper than we are used to in the West. It is not about the company or the name on the sign. It's about the people."

Putting it into action

1 **Build personal relationships alongside professional interactions.** Remember that in most Asian cultures, team members will not be loyal to you simply because of your title. Loyalty is primarily toward people, not companies. Take a genuine interest in them as individuals, make small talk, share personal information about yourself. Keep it professional, but make it clear you view them as more than just a company asset.

2 **Build a strong core of local people who can be honest with you.** Find people you can ask: "What should I do? What did that mean? What do you think?" People who you can trust to give you open and frank advice rather than merely polite responses. Find these outside of your direct team, reports or bosses.

3 **Join activities where locals and Westerners mix.** Some suggestions are team sports (dragon-boating, squash ladder, five-a-side, softball games), sports followers groups (a football team supporters bar, a live showing of a big game), arts groups, cooking classes, etc. These are good avenues for building relationships outside of work in a relaxed setting.

④ **Find out beforehand the networks of relationships that are in play – above and beyond the org chart.** Ahead of your first engagement with a new company, team, supplier, client or partner, ask your close contacts for pertinent background information on the new people. Ask specially about the relationships at play (hierarchies, alignments, rivalries, etc). You will need to be overt in your questioning, as they may take the relationships in place for granted and forget you are not aware of them.

⑤ **Take special care when inheriting a role from a predecessor.** If they had strong and positive relationships, that's a good start, but you must ensure you are able to transition them to you smoothly and build on them. If the relationships were not so good, try meeting with the other parties to show your commitment to a fresh start. Make it clear that you understand the past and want to build a stronger future. Be candid – ask what you can do personally to improve things.

⑥ **Decide early on whether you want to be social media "friends" with work contacts.** Many Asian cultures blur the lines between professional and personal social media use. Whether you choose to "friend" your work contacts or not, you need to be consistent. "Friending" no one is your choice. "Friending" some and not others could be seen as a snub.

⑦ **Map out 10 key relationships inside your organisation and outside it.** Identify which ones you already have and how strong they are (be honest), and which ones you don't have yet but need to build. Set yourself the goal of doing something to strengthen those relationships every week. Send them the link to an article you feel may interest them. Drop by their office to say hello. Suggest going for a coffee. Then build on the list to identify your 50 key relationships. Find a reason at least one a month to connect with these people.

8 **Invest in relationships for the long term.** Remember that building strong relationships can take years. Don't be impatient. This is a marathon, not a sprint. Build relationships with people regardless of whether you think you will need help or agreement from them. The full network of relationships is often invisible at first. These people may hold soft power that you will rely on later.

9 **Make relationship-building a daily habit.** Invest time on a day-to-day level in making small talk, socialising and engaging. If necessary, build it into your diary, with a reminder alert. Soon it will become second nature to you.

2:
Power

"In Asia you only know
where the power is when
you find yourself sat next to it."
— Andrew, Asia-Pacific regional
director, 10 years in Asia

"I came to Asia back in '91. We were the last generation of 'international officer corps' bank management trainees sent out from Britain to the colonies – in our case, Hong Kong. The job description hadn't changed much in a century and could be summed up as 'stop the locals stealing the cash'. We were told not to loiter outside the bank to smoke. The 'powers that be' believed a group of white people standing outside the bank might make the locals think we knew something was up and were queuing up to pull out our money, and that it would cause a financial panic."

I'm talking to Mark, a 30-year Asia financial sector veteran. He actually has more of the bearing of a military officer than a banker. With his angular frame and measured movements, I can easily picture him in khaki, stick under his arm, walking ahead of a regiment. A generation earlier, that is probably what would have brought him here. It is an image I find hard to shake off once it is planted in my mind.

We are sitting at a high table in a coffee shop in a large mall, located under a major financial hub. It is large and airy, but there is no natural light and the footsteps of passersby reverberate. Mark continues:

"The world was changing – had changed – but the institutions and some of the individuals within them really hadn't. Or maybe they didn't want to see the change.

When I graduated to my full role, there was a ceremony, very grand. Some of the old-timers (they were in their 20s!) actually gave us a roasting. They felt we had been too familiar with the locals. We were told: 'What are you doing fraternising with the natives (the people we worked with and had trained with!)? You are the boss. Don't mess with the hierarchy.'

It was a colonial construct, an anachronism, but it had survived that long. In some people and some institutions, the delusion still carries on. It was – is – incredible. A set of people and institutions operating in a parallel reality. There are fewer of them now, but I still bump into some of them these days. They are on boards and committees. They are still out here.

Asia is now clearly playing by its own rules. In fact it has always done so. Many Westerners and Western companies were just too blinded by our delusions of power to see it. People still seem to think the Chinese are learning English because they want to emulate us. It's not. It's so they can understand

*us and be more effective when they do business with us or
manage us.*

*Western arrogance perpetuates this misinterpretation of
the facts. At best we are in a state of equality between East
and West – this is what we want to believe. But I believe Asian
dominance, and the implementation of that power, is inevita-
ble. I left the West 30 years ago for this very reason."*

In this chapter, we are talking about overt, institutional power.
The company boss. (There is of course a softer, invisible power
at play too. The power that those without obvious authority can
exert on a situation is explored in the chapter on Relationships.
There is also a power dynamic present within the Asian family
structure, which is often, but not always, paternal. This is discussed in the chapter on Family.)

The "boss" has a significantly larger impact in Asia than
the West. The pivotal role that the boss is perceived to play in
an Asian individual's finances, career, social status and overall
well-being is sometimes hard for a Westerner to grasp. The
power is culturally reinforced, socially accepted and so deeply
ingrained as to be unconsciously acted upon.

A study by Sook-Lei Liew, Yina Ma, Shihui Han and Lisa
Aziz-Zadeh, entitled "Who's Afraid of the Boss: Cultural Differences in Social Hierarchies Modulate Self-Face Recognition in
Chinese and Americans", clearly demonstrates what had until
recently been omnipresent but often invisible. This is what they
found.

When people are flashed an image of a person's face,
they unconsciously process and respond to it. By using
scrambled images, image placement and eye-tracking, it is

possible to measure, in nanoseconds, which images get the faster response. The faster the unconscious response, the more relevant or important that person is to the viewer.

It had already been established that people react to their own faces faster than to the faces of others. That makes sense: no matter how much we speak of altruism, deep down we need to look out for ourselves. Understandably, too, the study found that people responded to images of friends and family members faster than to those of strangers, and the closer the relationship, the faster the response.

This is interesting, but it gets really interesting when the subjects were flashed an image of their supervisor (boss). People overall responded to the boss image quicker than to the images of their friends and family. This has become known as the "boss effect": we unconsciously react quicker to our boss than to our friends and family.

The respondents were later broken out by background, Chinese versus American. While the Americans responded in the same way as the previous studies, the Asians were found to respond to the image of their bosses faster than their own image! Their boss was more important to them than they themselves were.

The team conducting the study concluded that understanding this difference is vital in light of globalisation, the prevalence of multicultural working environments, cross-country public policy and economic interdependence.

The difference in the level of power held and displayed by "the boss(es)" is clear in an example from Mark's time working with Western/Asian financial institutions.

"A Japanese company bought part of the bank I worked for. They were keen to strengthen their relationship with China and wanted to show they could work with them. So for the first big meeting between the Japanese bank and the Chinese, they sent me, the Westerner. They wanted to show that this was a meeting of equals. In their minds I was the big gun to be wheeled out.

In that first meeting, I was the only Westerner in a room of about 50 people. There were several layers of formal hierarchy. The Chinese singled me out immediately and directed every question at me. In Mandarin.

I was mortified. If they wanted to watch me squirm, it worked. They did it to convey a message loud and clear to my Japanese bosses. The message was: 'The Chinese are in charge. The power structure has not been observed properly here. You should have come yourself rather than think the Westerner was appropriate in your place. You should know your position in this relationship, and if you want to do business with us you'd better have some senior bankers who are Mandarin speakers.'

The message was received and understood!

When an Asian business buys up a Western one, the Western team have to adapt quickly to the new owner's ways of working. Particularly if the part they bought isn't doing as well as expected. Pretty soon the buyer decides they can't work with the people they bought, particularly any that rankle or upset the buyer's status quo. The people who are not a good cultural fit are gone. I spent a lot of time with the Tokyo management team who'd bought us. Many Western colleagues did not, and in a couple of years they were gone.

*The cracks are obvious to anyone who is paying atten-
tion, but many Westerners are resting on their 'colonial laurels'.
Non-conformers are seen as damaging the broader culture of
the firm, but they may be kept on board if they pull their weight.
In the end, though, no level of performance will justify ongoing
cultural disruption."*

People who don't fit into the new cultural norm but are making
good money for the buyer will be tolerated for a while. But as
soon as the financials hit a bump, these people are gone.

Whilst the anecdotal evidence is compelling, it is worth
taking the time to consider the theory that underpins it. We
should look closely at the different types of power and the different ways in which power is manifested.

As mentioned in the Introduction, the anthropologist
Edward Hall originally proposed the mapping of cultures across
a low-context and high-context axis. This has remained the
foundation of thinking on the subject ever since.

In general, low-context cultures (mainly in the West) tend
to have flatter power structures. The relationships are more
equal, and people of different power and status levels interact more. This, building on Hall's thinking, is referred to as
low power distance. These behaviours are seen more often in
Western countries.

High-context cultures have high power distance. These
cultures (Asia) have much more hierarchical power structures.
It is clear who the bosses are, and they have a disproportion-
ate amount of power versus those under them. People will be
more fixed in their status band and there is less possibility of
an individual moving between the levels in a project context.

People occupying different levels will have limited professional or social interaction. Social and professional mobility may also be low.

People in cultures with high power distance tend to display their power roles overtly and expect them to be acknowledged. The boss will be smartly dressed, often with expensive accessories, which clearly displays their success and status.

The world's largest market for luxury watches is China. Which is ironic, as (discussed in the chapter on Time) people in Asia don't appear to use them to actually track time very often!

Titles are expected to be used (Mr, Dr, Director, Sir), and people will expect to be treated with the respect due to their position. Senior figures are listened to and are rarely contradicted or interrupted. Behaviour around the bosses is usually formal, restrained and measured. You don't joke around with the boss.

In such cultures, it is very clear who is in charge, so decisions can get made quickly and actions get implemented fast. People know their roles and what they are expected to do. Little time is wasted on debate or discussion, so things can get done. This is a positive outcome of the high power distance.

On the other hand, new ideas are often not heard and suggestions are rarely given. Juniors are not listened to or encouraged to participate.

That said, in recent years there have been changes to hierarchical norms in China regarding the role and visibility of "junior staff". With the one-child policy resulting in a shortage of skilled younger professionals joining large organisations, and diminishing levels of company loyalty, big companies are fighting over young talent. As a result, younger team members with less experience are being encouraged to participate more in discussions, voice their opinions and even offer dissenting views. The belief is that empowering these younger people will help retain them, whereas treating them in the traditional manner will drive them away. It is too early to tell if this is working.

This aside, most decisions are still made behind closed doors by senior management with little transparency or opportunities for wider discussion. The brains, experience and perspective of the full team are hence often left untapped.

People in cultures with low power distance (the West) will often try their best not to look or act like the boss. Meetings proceed more like conversations, with leaders encouraging the sharing of thoughts and ideas. Interaction is less formal and it may be hard for an observer to quickly recognise where the actual power in a group lies. People tend to refer to each other by their first names, and the relationships and engagements are less formal and structured.

This encourages the sharing of ideas, thoughts and builds, and can lead to the development of better solutions together. But it also slows down decision-making. Whilst it may give the appearance of equality, a single decision still needs to be made ultimately. Someone still needs to make the final call.

Mark's insights into overt power displays remind me of one of my first projects in Asia, working for a global luxury spirits company. We were working downstream from a big, very sexy, very cool UK-based innovation agency, helping to develop and execute the ideas for a new range of high-end spirits they were generating for the client. It was a big, high-profile project for the innovation agency and it would help cement their relationship with the client and build their credibility in Asia. I was working for a design agency, and our role was to add in some design strategy and then execute the ideas.

As part of the collaboration, we were invited along to the innovation workshop. It was being run by the innovation agency's hot, young, cool kids. A huge amount of research, insight generation and preparation had been done already. They had flown out from London to the client's office in Hong Kong for the workshop.

The innovation team lived up to expectations. They had their own bespoke process, they had their own jargon, they had ripped jeans and ironic haircuts. From the moment we stepped into the conference room that was being used for the session, it was clear they were in charge.

We were part of *their* process, *their* way of working. They had total self-confidence in what they were doing and in their abilities. They immediately started telling everyone where to sit, to put away their laptops, phones – including the client team. I didn't know it at the time, but that's when the red flags should have started to go up!

Yes, they were the subject matter experts, but they hadn't factored in, at all, that no matter how good they were, they were still the vendor. The client – and specifically the marketing director, the most senior person from their side present – was really in charge. And it was important that he was seen to be.

The morning went smoothly, following the prescribed process. I was having a great time. Post-it notes, whiteboards, great stuff! Then a buffet lunch was brought into the room. We ate and chatted.

That's when it all started going wrong for them.

After lunch was a re-energiser exercise, an activity intended to help shake off the mid-afternoon slump, keep energy levels up, get us moving again. It was star jumps.

We had to do 10 each. I don't know if you know what a star jump is? You drop down to the floor in the press-up position, quickly pull your legs forward to your chest, and then pop up into a jump, and throw your hands up and outward, making a star shape. Not the hardest thing in the world if you are relatively fit, but physically stretching if you're not.

The client team's marketing director was a little older than the rest of those present. He carried himself with the gravity of someone with a senior role in a global luxury goods company. He wore a handmade, tailored suit. A large and expensive watch. He had the physicality of someone who spent a lot of time sitting in meetings, enjoyed long lunches, fine wines and cigars. The paunch did not communicate "Hey, I'm the kind of man that does a lot of star jumps".

At the innovation team's direction, we all dropped down to press-up position. The marketing director didn't budge. They encouraged him in a good-natured manner. He still didn't budge. He had to retain his position of power, to not allow the vendor to tell him what to do – especially not something so undignified.

Meanwhile, the agency lead felt he had to keep control of the workshop process. They were running it. They were in charge. This was their room.

Eventually the rest of us were excused and asked to go for coffee. When we returned a few minutes later, the notion of star jumps had evaporated. We started the next activity, and after about 30 minutes the marketing director excused himself for an "urgent call". He never came back, and the workshop finished a little early.

A few days later, we found out that we would be taking the lead on the project going forward. The innovation agency's work up to that point was handed to us, and we moved forward with the creative development. That was good news for us, but not so good for the innovation agency. The power had always been with the client, and a bunch of scruffy kids from England were not going to undermine that status.

As you will see elsewhere in this book, rarely is a culture or individual operating at the extreme ends of the Asia/West axis; they diverge from the central point in different ways, and to varying extents. However, a hip, informal, flat-structured Western innovation team and a formal, hierarchical, image-conscious Asian luxury goods company are clearly two paradigms at pretty much opposite ends of the scale.

To outsiders, some protocols may be baffling or appear unnecessary – ridiculous even – but in fact they all have a vital importance in ensuring the smooth running of the power dynamic in a high-context culture. The rituals and protocols make it clear where the power sits. These overt displays of power can be very useful in giving a Westerner directions on how to behave in return.

The final word on this topic comes from Karsten, our good friend the diplomat, who we hear from in-depth in the chapter on Time Perception. Karsten has clear insight into the level of influence that power gives in Asia:

"The boss has a much greater amount of direct and indirect power here than in the West. The boss' words are loaded with

power. Even as a Western boss here in Asia, my words can make things happen. Changes I want to make – to policy, to people – which would take a long time and a whole process in the West, I can achieve here with a few well-timed and well-chosen comments."

Putting it into action

1 **Before meeting an individual or a group, find out where the power lies.** Do your research. Check social media, the website of the company, ask friendly sources. Identify who wields the real power in the organisation.

2 **On entering a room, acknowledge the most powerful people first.** Act with deference and respect. Do not "play it cool". No one will be impressed by your show of being unimpressed. The powerful will feel disrespected and the others present will simply feel you are tone-deaf to the situation and the protocols.

3 **To make a good first impression, err on the side of formality.** Titles and designations are used to good effect in high-context cultures. On being introduced, shake hands and give a formal greeting. Business cards should be passed and received one at a time with both hands, with a pause to look at the card as a mark of respect.

4 **Always wait for the person with power to arrive before starting a meeting.** And be prepared to wait. The most powerful person will usually be the last to arrive. Don't try and start without them present – it will be perceived as grievously rude. In any case, if you do start the meeting without them, you will likely have to repeat everything when they do arrive. While waiting for the boss, engage with those already present. It's an invaluable opportunity to build connections. Do not just read emails or stare at your phone; get to know your potential allies and advocates.

⑤ **At the start of the meeting, acknowledge that you do not speak the language of the majority of those present.** Thank them for taking the trouble to work in a second language. A self-deprecating comment and apology will make it clear that you do not think they should have to speak your language, and that you are grateful if they do.

⑥ **Dress the part – usually more formally than in an equivalent Western business situation.** "Casual power" style has not reached Asia yet. If you have – or wish to appear to have – a position of power and influence, you need to dress and behave accordingly. This doesn't have to mean a three-piece suit, but smart, new, pressed, clean and sharp is the minimum. You can be flamboyant, but not scruffy.

⑦ **Avoid joking behaviour.** If you want to be taken seriously, you need to behave seriously. Joking behaviour undermines authority and will likely backfire.

⑧ **Be careful what you ask for.** If you are in a position of power in Asia, an offhand comment from you may often be taken as a direct order or request. Remarks like "I wonder what that would look like in blue" or "I sometimes get peckish in the late afternoon" may mean someone working late on a blue version of whatever you had been looking at, and sandwiches appearing in your office at 4 pm every day from then on.

3:
Family

"You need to
acknowledge the
central place of the
family and the roles,
responsibilities and
expectations within it."
— Peter Ter Kulve, President,
Unilever Home Care

There is a Chinese saying, "The falling leaf returns to the roots that sired it".

Most of the five vital relationships promoted by Confucius are family ones. The majority of Chinese adults, if they don't remain living at "home" with their parents, will continue to live in the same village or neighbourhood. Adults that need to spend periods of time away during their working lives will usually return to their home town or village when they get older.

In Japan, two-thirds of households are intergenerational. Indian families are also very close-knit and have large kinship networks and a value orientation that places family at the heart of all matters. Many families will live multi-generationally in the same home, but even when they live in separate dwellings, visits home are frequent and expected.

The importance of family – even family members not directly connected to the business – is something Peter is very aware of. Peter is Global President of Unilever Home Care and has spent several years working across their Asia offices.

I walk through a large open-plan space to meet him. A diverse mix of young professionals huddle over co-working tables, peer intently at laptop screens, stride purposefully from one meeting to another. There are brightly coloured walls, open kitchen spaces, whiteboards. These are global marketers in their natural habitat.

Peter has the corner office. His inner sanctum is sparse but thoughtful. A desk and laptop. A few well-chosen mementos and framed family pictures. Large windows overlook the other shiny high-rises, and in the distance is a sliver of sea view.

"In Asia I led a lot of acquisitions – a lot of big, family-owned businesses. Family-owned and family-led companies have a very different dynamic from more corporate organisations. To work with, compete with or acquire these companies, you need to understand that dynamic.

We are used to clear-cut structures – CEO, Board, Chairman. With a family-owned company, the power structure and relationships are not always so clear. You need to take time to understand and then to navigate that landscape. You need to understand the different views, the different objectives within the family, and the key relationships you need to build.

Whilst all this seems more complex, it is actually more stable. The family is in place for generations. They will often find it confusing working with us, because from their perspective, our key people and structure change so often."

Peter speaks with a Dutch accent, which makes his speech crisp. The words have edges to them. His accent actually makes him easier to follow than a native English speaker. With his shaved head, blue jeans and tailored Italian shirts, Peter is crisp and clear. Like his speech.

"This makes long-term relationship-building very important. I led a joint venture with a family-owned company in Myanmar. For the first three years the family didn't even want to meet me. Then eventually we had a lunch, at which no one admitted to speaking English. A year later, another lunch. Finally, after five years, serious conversations started with the different branches of the family. I'm still Chairman of that joint venture.

Another time, we had a bright young guy in our Singapore team. We found him a really good role in Vietnam. A step up for him. But his mother blocked it. She thought it would be too dangerous. So to get past that, we sent them on a trip to Ho Chi Minh City together, so she could see it first-hand. She was reassured. He moved.

Once I was on an Outward Bound trip with my team. We were crossing a high ridge when I had an attack of vertigo. It was scary. I turned to our Financial Director, an Asian woman, who was next to me, and said, 'At least if I go over the edge, it will be just me, and quick!' She replied, 'If I go over the edge, my whole family will fall with me. I support them all.'

On another occasion, I was leading the purchase of a large family-owned Indonesian company. One day, during a meeting, the family patriarch turned to me and said, 'I could sell to you, but I don't know what to do with the money and I worry about my sons. They both have solid jobs with the company. When I get my millions, what will they do? I don't want them being venture capitalists, I want them to have proper jobs, to be grounded, not to be flash.'

That is the multi-generational aspect of the family business."

In the West, we expect family to play a diminishing role in our lives as we get older. Young children rely 100% on their parents for food, shelter and emotional support. As they get older, teachers and friends become bigger influences. Inevitably, people leave home in their late teens or early 20s and return with decreasing frequency as they get older, until eventually they have children themselves, and the cycle repeats.

Western family relationships – and particularly how children interact with their parents – is seen as shocking, and even shameful, by many Asians.

In a 2017 paper, Parul Bhandari and Fritzi-Marie Titzmann looked at numerous studies on the role of family in South Asia ("Family Realities in South Asia: Adaptations and Resilience"). They noted that the family plays a pivotal role in both the reality and the imagination of individuals and groups. It is the crucial building block of identity. Family structures shape the norms of behaviour – from gender roles to career choices – and lead to social, technological and cultural changes.

In collectivist societies (as opposed to Western individualistic ones), the family is the emotional and economic support system. The family takes care of the young and the very old, provides comfort and assistance to widows and (traditionally) the older unmarried. It supports individuals during times of unemployment and illness. It also provides long-term support for the disabled. In Asia there are few retirement homes; older people live within the extended family.

Max is German. He came to Asia for a performing arts festival (he's a fire juggler), where he met another performer, a Singaporean, and they fell in love. He followed his heart, and without a job or a plan, he packed his bags and jumped on plane to be with her. Now Max is the founder of a very successful startup. He is making a lot of noise in the tech space and they have attracted serious investment. Sometimes you have to leap before you look.

"I fell in love with a girl and moved here and lived with a Chinese family. I see things differently from most expats.

The global success of Asian countries such as Singapore, South Korea and China is a reflection of how their family structure works. It makes me question whether the Western view of what is fundamental is right. Free speech, democracy – yes, they are systems within a strong and solid nation, but I think they are aspects that can be introduced once the nation is strong and secure. They don't work when dropped into a country before it is ready.

A benevolent dictator – that's who builds a country quickly. It's like back when a king or an emperor ruled a country. They were trained from birth to be a just leader, and most of the time they were. Their focus was on what was best for the country – maybe not for some individuals or for smaller groups, but for the country overall.

This is the country reflecting the family structure. A single benevolent matriarch or patriarch that works hard and wants the best for their family. An extended family that understands their roles and follows directions. Everyone pulling together for the common good.

Democracy may help sustain a successful country – it gives a degree of control to the people and prevents despots – but at some point it stops working. Now our leaders don't have that ability to lead. We don't elect the ones best equipped for the job. Elections have become popularity contests.

One thing I have seen in Asia is that status is defined by your place in the pyramid. You move up by age and experience, and once you are up a level, you are isolated from the ones below. In the West, it's more fluid. You need to continually defend and re-establish your place in the pyramid. In Asia, once you move up a rung, that is where you stay. As in the family, same in society."

The family hierarchy structure is much stricter in Asia than in the West. There are specific terms used to describe the level of respect to be shown to different family members. An uncle that is the older brother of the father ranks higher than an uncle that is the younger brother, for example.

Within the family unit, children are expected to obey their parents. Not just when they are young, but right into adulthood. Parents will make choices on which subjects to study at school, which college to go to, which job to apply for, which offer to accept. Do not be surprised if a local colleague or friend mentions that they are asking for their parents' advice, guidance or even permission on a decision.

It is usually the patriarch that is the clear head of the family. They will make the decisions on a wide range of topics, many of which in the West we would balk at our parents making for us. A person's deference to their parents continues even after they become parents themselves.

In China, the phrase "Family is life" is often heard and definitely believed. Many Eastern religious philosophies, as well as the writings of Confucius mentioned earlier, emphasise the central role of family. Each member – husband, wife, eldest son, eldest daughter, elder brother, etc – has clear roles and responsibilities. There are also very specific rules governing the interaction between parents and children, husband and wife.

It's hard to imagine from a Western viewpoint, but the majority of marriages in the world are arranged ones (53% according to a Statistic Brain study). These range from highly formal arranged marriages, in which the couple have little to no choice in the matter, to more informal arrangements involving well-meaning, but insistent, introductions by relatives.

An arranged marriage is not necessarily an unwilling one. Many young people are reported to believe that such an important decision should be made by their parents or elders. They know their parents want the best for them and trust the decision. In India, Pakistan, Bangladesh and parts of Southeast Asia, most married people you meet will have met their partner through an arranged match. The continued dominance of and preference for arranged marriages is a powerful demonstration of the influence that family has on individuals.

In the West, choosing your life partner is probably the single most important decision we ever make. And it is primarily an individual decision. Is this person right for me? Does this person make me happy? Do I make them happy? Do I trust this person? Do I want to have children with this person? Do I want to grow old with them?

Because it is so important, it is vital that it is right for us and what we want. So it is a decision primarily made by that individual. In Asia, the importance of the decision is exactly why it *isn't* made by the individual. It needs to be considered in the widest possible terms. Does the potential life partner come from a good family? What is their history? Can the husband support the wife? What are the social and business implications? Such a weighty decision should be made by older, wiser people, not left to two young people giddy with emotions and hormones.

How the West and Asia treat older people is also very different, and instructive in many ways. In most Eastern cultures, the elders of a family are revered. In the West, we often take our parents and grandparents for granted or, worse, disregard them.

In the East, elders are seen as a source of wisdom born of experience. They have seen more and done more than the younger generations. They should be turned to for counsel and guidance. In the West, we miss out on this huge resource. In Asia, too, grandparents will often take an active role in raising grandchildren, allowing overstretched parents to focus on work and each other.

Max tells of his experience:

"When my mother came to stay with us in Singapore, my mother-in-law insisted on my mother having the best bed in the house – which was her bed! My mother, through politeness,

couldn't accept; my mother-in-law, through politeness, had to insist.

I think the strength of family ties is due partly to the distance from poverty. In Asia, a lot of families, even successful ones, are still just one generation from poverty. It is a real, live memory. Because of that, they realise the importance of the family as a safety net that is there in times of trouble. So they make sure to keep it strong.

In the West, most of us are multiple generations away from real poverty. We don't feel vulnerable or exposed, so we no longer feel such a keen need to have family around us.

Here, most people are still living in multi-generational environments. And it's great! Having people to help, to support. The conflict between work and kids is alleviated. The younger generation can go out and earn and bring value back into the family, whilst the older people look after the home and care for the kids. Everyone has a valid and valued role. It works.

That's where the West falls flat. Older people are redundant and excluded. Younger people are then left trying to juggle work and family. If you don't work hard and bring home a good wage, you're a failure. But if you don't spend enough quality time with your kids, you're a failure too! It's impossible to deliver both. It's a no-win situation.

Then we ask why the Western population is dropping. Why don't millennials buy into the system? Why aren't they driven? Well, who wants that?!

When you remember poverty, you want to protect your children and grandchildren from it. You make decisions based not on what is best for you, but what is best for the future. In the West, most people have no memory of suffering or hardship, *and that means they can't imagine it in the future. They make decisions and take actions that benefit only them, in the now. We see that in how Asia is pursuing a strategy of long-term change, whereas the West is chasing short-term gratification."*

There are some unexpected effects of intergenerational living, too. Rebecca, a regional agency head, gives us a telling story. Rebecca competes in vertical marathons (racing up the stairs of Asian skyscrapers) and has run large sections of the Great Wall. She is focused and ambitious – at play and at work. With an infectious smile and the remnants of a Down Under accent (diluted by 15 years away from home), she puts people at ease.

"I arrived in Singapore as the manager for a small team and learned quickly that they were all working ludicrous hours, after 10 pm most nights. Being new, I made the decision to get 'in the trenches' with them and build trust with them. We slogged into the night. We ate local hawker meals together in the evening and sacrificed our evening time at the altar of the computer screen.

A month into the job and my boss reported that she was receiving a lot of compliments. My team were happy and impressed by the angmoh (slang for Westerner). But, given that I was working the same late-night hours plus weekends, I wasn't feeling so happy myself!

I decided that it was time to do something bold but positive on behalf of the team – by improving their work/life balance. I would start pushing back with clients and bosses. I declared that if there was anyone in the team still working after 7 pm then we, together, had failed.

Soon after this announcement, though, my boss reported that she was getting complaints from my team. They were no longer happy working under my leadership, and some were even asking to switch teams. What was going on?

It took me another few weeks to realise my mistake. By asking the team to leave the office by 7 pm, I was essentially forcing them to go home to their parents! I was also taking away the perk of a paid-for meal with their friends and a taxi home after 8 pm. They were all 20-somethings still living at home, and if they didn't need to be in the office then they would have to find another reason to not be at home. A reason that would require them to pay for their own entertainment and food.

What a bitch to take this away from them!

Once I finally figured this out, we set new rules. I was happy to take the morning shift but I would not work past 7 pm. I would, however, still sign off their taxi and meal expenses. I was no longer in the trenches with the team, but a more acceptable order had been set."

Aside from the irritation for young people of having to go home to face their parents every night, in Asia the family clearly remains the primary unit. It is more important than the individual. It is the universal structure, an institution to be cherished and respected.

In the West, we seem to have discarded a lot of the benefits of family in our quest for self-determinism. I am my own boss. Judge me on my own merits – as I will judge others. I make my own decisions and stand or fall by them. There are benefits to this, but also costs. We struggle to juggle family and work. We lose out on the wisdom, experience and support of our elders. We are more isolated and alone than ever before. Of course, the extended family has its challenges too, but have we in the West thrown away too much for too little?

The last word goes to Max:

"Back in the West, family relationships beyond your immediate family are merely transactional. What am I supposed to do? How much time do I need to spend with this person?

In Asia, the larger family, they will do anything for each other. Nothing is too much trouble. Even a relative you have only ever met once, they would rip off an arm and a leg for you."

Putting it into action

1 **See the family behind the individual.** When an Asian colleague or friend mentions they are still living at home or they need to seek agreement from a parent on a key decision, be careful not to make assumptions. In the West, this may seem indicative of a lack of maturity, but that impression is wholly Western-centric. The scenario has a completely different meaning in Asia. It is reflection of the culture, not the person's character, independence or ambition.

2 **Be empathetic about family pressure on your team members.** Apart from the pressure of expectations, there could be very real financial pressure as well. One person may be the sole breadwinner supporting an entire extended family. In

these situations, professional instability or risk can be hugely worrying to them. Their whole family may be relying on the extra income from a promotion or a bonus. Being fired or made redundant can be devastating. I'm not suggesting people should be rewarded for under-delivering, but be mindful of the repercussions.

③ Don't try and pin people down on an individual decision. Asians are not obsessed with individual determinism like the West is, but allow themselves to flow with the group, under the direction of the authority figure. Build the need for alignment with this figure into decision-making processes. Give people space to get that input, and ensure time is allocated for this decision stage.

④ Make sure you are aware of any family relationships in your team, company, client contacts, etc. Ask your trusted contacts. Check social media. People having the same surname does not mean they are related. But not having the same surname does not mean they are not! Being aware of relationships, hierarchies and power structures is always important in Asia, but making sure you are on top of the family links is vital. An inadvertent comment to the wrong person can wreak havoc.

⑤ Don't make assumptions about the abilities of an individual based on their family relationship with other team members. You may find yourself working with multiple generations of a family, siblings and in-laws in the same company. You should not interpret this as underhand behaviour. Do not think you have unearthed a secret. The relationship will be public knowledge. Being a family member is an added benefit to an appointment; rarely is it the key criteria. So be aware of the relationships in place, but do not allow them to colour your opinion of individuals.

6 **Allow flexibility for family time.** Asian team members and colleagues will make frequent and extended visits home. In the West, this often means a family crisis or death has occurred. In Asia it is simply normal behaviour. Be aware of this and ensure flexibility for your teams.

7 **Allow flexibility for time away from the family.** Some younger Asian people may want to work late, or at least remain in the office under the guise of working. Their home may be multigenerational, where they may have little privacy from the prying eyes of family. Whilst we may be eager to escape the office, it is possible that members of an Asian team may want to stay. Don't assume you need to stay as long as them, or expect them to leave as early as you do.

4:
Gender

"In Asia, the gender
expectations placed on
men and women are even
more confusing, challenging
and contradictory than in the
West. I didn't think that was
possible until I got here and
saw it." — Zeina, construction
project manager, 12 years in Asia

Gender is an emotive, confusing and contentious topic. It is a very visible manifestation of the cultural convergence between Asia and the West.

I remember presenting to the senior team of a big local company in Cambodia. The CEO, CMO, CFO and what looked to be all of their direct reports were sitting at a long conference table in a big old-school meeting room. Me at one end with laptop and projector. The usual dance.

Part-way through the session, an older woman quietly entered the room carrying a tea tray. The meeting stopped, and everyone jumped up to greet her. "Wow," I thought, "these guys are really nice to the tea lady. What a great bunch!" She slowly went round the table, made a little small talk with each person, served them tea and moved along. She got to me, smiled, I smiled, she gave me a cup of tea and then took her leave. After she left, everyone turned back to me, and the presentation resumed.

It was only afterwards, over dinner, that I found out she was the family matriarch. The late founder's wife. Mother of the CEO and CMO! She had always been the driver of the business, leading from behind her husband. In a culture where a smart and ambitious woman wasn't allowed to run a business, she ran it through her men. Each little piece of small talk as she went around had been a definite question, an update or a decision.

I had no clue.

But this situation, whilst not unique, is in no way wholly representative of reality. Millions of women in Asia face challenges that are hard for us to grasp in the West. In many countries they are still seen as second-class citizens. They grow up with less access to education, have lower exposure to opportunities and are less able to follow their own interests or make the most of their talents.

The World Economic Forum's 2018 gender pay gap survey ranked a number of Asian countries poorly. Out of 149 countries surveyed, Japan came in at 103, South Korea at 110, and China at 115.

In 2018 a prestigious Japanese medical school was found to be rigging its entrance procedures against women in order to ensure a higher number of male doctors. They claimed this was to help counter the negative impact of many female doctors quitting the profession early to have children.

Research by McKinsey in 2018 ("The Power of Parity: Advancing Women's Equality in Asia Pacific") estimated that

Southeast Asia's economy would be boosted by US$370 trillion per year by 2025 if the existing inequality between the genders was eliminated.

It would be easy to conclude that differences in gender roles in Asia are simply an indication of a societal time lag compared to the West. Men are still the primary providers – they focus on their careers and are masters of their home – while women play a secondary role, focusing on children and housekeeping, and if they do work, occupy lower-level jobs. Asia now is simply what the West was like 30 years ago and they need to catch up with us.

It would be easy to think this, but it would be wrong.

Yes, Asian societal structures may in many ways seem 30 years out of date to us, but cultural, economic and professional expectations and norms have radically moved forward – to be in line with, or even ahead of, the West.

Men have very demanding roles, as sons, fathers and brothers. There are very specific behaviours expected in terms of filial and family responsibility. There are rigid and often unrealistic demands that parents put on sons to achieve at school, at university and in the workplace. Sons are seen not only as the providers for their own family unit (wife and children), but are also expected to be the financial providers and safety net for parents as they get older.

Men are expected to not just achieve professionally, but also follow the visible rules and indications of the drive for that success. Late nights at the office. Working weekends. Socialising every night with the boss.

Men are expected to be solid, stoic, uncomplaining. As we in the West might put it, they have to "man up".

On top of these traditional demands, they now also have another – often competing – set of expectations to fulfil. Be a good husband. Ensure a healthy and happy relationship with your wife and help out at home. Be a good father, spend quality time with your kids, helping them learn, encouraging them. Be open and in touch with your emotions.

These competing demands may seem familiar to a Western man, but in the West, these changes have happened slowly over decades. Whilst there is some overlap and conflict from the competing expectations, mostly one set of expectations has slowly been replaced by the other. In the East, these changing expectations have emerged over a much shorter time period. The two sets of competing demands are now operating simultaneously.

Global culture promotes individual responsibility and accountability for men, at a younger and younger age. But in the East, sons will defer to their fathers' wishes much longer than may seem normal to us. In many cases, the father will remain the final authority and decision-maker, right up to his death. Decisions that we would expect an adult to make on their own will very often need to be checked with the patriarch – educational choices, career moves, even things like major purchases.

This does not make an Asian man less decisive, competent, masculine or authoritative than his Western counterpart. It merely reflects the different societal structure and expectations. But it does add an extra level of complication – of competing pressures and expectations – to his life.

These competing forces similarly, but more pointedly, affect women too.

Asian cultures generally still expect women to be the primary caregivers for children. To undertake almost all of the household chores, and to be the carers for ageing parents. But simultaneously, changing societal expectations and the economic realities of 21st-century life mean most women are working full-time too. Society expects women to increasingly act and be seen as equal to men – at home and in the workplace. But, just as in the case of men's roles, culture has not adjusted the expectations. This means women's traditional role (home, parents, children) has not changed to make space for the increased new demands.

The result is a generation of Asian women who are being pulled in two or more directions. Yes, this is similar to the challenges faced by women in the West – but again the difference in Asia is the speed of the change.

The inconsistency of gender roles and conflicting demands on individuals come into sharp relief in interactions between men and women, particularly across status levels.

Zeina is a project manager in the construction industry. A female "boss" in a traditionally male-dominated business. She has been in Asia for 10 years and has some valuable learnings on balancing gender expectations and the Asia/West convergence.

"On one early project I worked on, I shouted at a lead contractor on a building site. I was swearing and telling him what he had done wrong, and generally acting like everyone on every building site I had ever worked on in Britain. You shout, you argue, you get the job done, you forget it, you all go to the pub as mates later. But the guy wasn't reacting the way he was

supposed to. He was frozen. He was horrified. He didn't know what to do."

Zeina and I are sitting in an office drinking tea. She apologises for being a little late. A minor administrative task earlier in the day had morphed into a huge – and in her opinion, wholly unnecessary – process. It becomes apparent that Zeina has little time for people who can't do their jobs. A viewpoint that caused her problems when she first came to Asia.

"Turns out Asia isn't the same as the UK. You can't blow up at people here. I had made myself look really bad. In the eyes of the onlookers, I had lost control. I had humiliated the male contractor and shown myself in a terrible light.

Consensus, harmony, discretion are the key words. Use the hierarchy, the process. It may take a little longer, but you will get things done. Resorting to Western sledgehammer tactics grinds everything to a halt.

I was also used to men and women working on an even footing. I was a woman publicly berating a man. This hit him a lot harder than I realised."

Zeina doesn't look like she spends her days on building sites. She is off-duty, so in a relaxed frame of mind and dress. She is wearing elegant but functional exercise gear, her dark hair pulled back into a ponytail. If I had to guess, I would have said she was a lifestyle coach, not a construction project manager.

"Public confrontations are often so mortifying to the locals that they freeze. They simply don't know what to do. They can't

give you the answer you don't want, and they can't lie to your face. So they say nothing. They just go silent. So you ask again. Nothing. Again. Nothing. It's ramping up and up. The more the local says nothing, the more annoyed the Westerner gets, so the more tense the confrontation becomes. Add in an embarrassing gender factor and it can be a nightmare.

Now, before I ask a question, I explain that whatever the answer is, it's fine. That we can work out the next steps regardless of what they say, and there won't be a problem. I really need to know the status of a project to be able to move forward in the right way. This way, they feel more comfortable sharing news that they may have been reluctant to tell me or admit to.

Be humble. Be a little self-deprecating. Throw in lots of praise when you are talking. Wrap your criticism with praise. Actually, we should probably do that wherever we are in the world!

I think that's why women often do so well here. We have more empathy than men. We are less likely to try and bully our way into getting the outcomes that we want. We are more likely to try and understand what the other person wants and needs.

I didn't have a clue when I got here. Now I see other people arrive and try to do things exactly the same way as at home. No matter how much you try to explain that it won't work, they don't listen. They have their baptism of fire, then hopefully by their second year they've got half an idea what they are doing!

What I try to do is to flatten out the hierarchy. At the start of a project, I make it clear that I am approachable, that I'm not going to go off on someone, but also that while I am a *woman, I am the boss. You can't remove the hierarchy – you don't want to – but you can acknowledge it and flatten it to not get in the way too much. Stay true to your word and you will earn the team's respect. Then they will be more open.*

But you need to acknowledge the hierarchy and the gender roles first. If you don't know they are there, or pretend you don't know, then you will be seen as just another Westerner who doesn't understand. You won't deserve any respect."

In Asia, gender interaction is often more controlled, more formalised. It discourages a lot of deliberate and accidental sexism. It opens up space for women to have senior roles, particularly in areas that are very male-dominated in the West. Project managers in the construction business in the UK are almost always men. Here in Singapore, Zeina informs me, she knows teams that are 50-50.

"Creating and policing that 'space' comes at a bit of a cost. Casual sexism is an absolute no-go here. There are laws which seem really strict compared to the West. I had a colleague who put his hand on the knee of a female co-worker. It was a casual thing, part of a 'thank you' for her agreeing to do something for him. She called the police. He was arrested. Same thing with another colleague. He was showing a female member of the team how to do something, and without thinking he put his hand on the small of her back. He was arrested. In both cases we had to suspend them until the cases were concluded."

These actions would have fallen under "outrage of modesty" – a blanket legal term for inappropriate behaviour. If the female victim is "outraged", then by definition what the man did is an offence. All parties need to be clear where the lines are.

Ray, a scientist based in Asia (who we hear more from in the chapter on Standing Out), sees a distinct under-representation of women at a senior level in his field.

"At a certain level of seniority, you stop seeing women in science here. But it's not through misogyny. It's risk aversion.

Appointing senior roles is risky. There is a lot of pressure to find the right person. How that appointee performs will reflect on you. So when looking at candidates, the 'low-risk' option is preferred. Familiarity minimises risk. The senior figures are middle-aged men. Middle-aged men know other middle-aged men. They were probably classmates, or in the army together, they have a shared history. They are safe options. In a highly risk-averse society, the safe option wins.

I haven't heard it said that women can't do the jobs. It's just safer to go with what – and who – you know."

We would be wise not to project our views onto other cultures and new situations. We should stop and think before we make decisions or form opinions of others based on our assumptions about their priorities or values. We should think about the gender roles and expectations in the cultures in which we are operating. Then, before making decisions or making statements, try and gather as much information about the real dynamics, the power structures and the expectations as possible.

Navneeta is a senior figure in the advertising industry. Like construction, advertising has traditionally been a bit of an "old boys' club" (we hear more from Navneeta in the chapter on Relationships). She adds another layer of insight around gender:

"You notice men in power – you know who they are. Women in power, particularly in Asia, are more difficult to spot and read. They have learnt to play their cards a little closer to their chest. In Asia they are often still learning how to implement that power. The subtlety comes from necessity.

As a Westernised senior professional Asian woman in an industry where most senior people are men, it can get very complicated. This particular combination is rare. People will tend to assume the white guy is the boss.

Sometimes it's hard to know how to act. Coming out of a meeting, two Western men would think nothing of going for a drink together. A white guy and a white woman probably would too. Two Asian guys are less likely to. Asian guy and Western woman? Almost certainly not. What are the dynamics for me then? I'm still working that out!"

Putting it into action

① **In matters of gender, err on the safe side.** Be aware of and follow social norms when interacting with the opposite sex. Even if you don't agree with them, follow them. If you are ever uncertain as to the right behaviour, be cautious and go with the safe option to avoid causing offence or being accused of impropriety.

2 **Be alert for the powerful women.** The women in the room may be more important than they appear. Do not assume that the person getting the most airtime is the most important person. Often women may have more senior roles, but protocol dictates that the men take the visible lead.

3 **Avoid public confrontations, particularly if it crosses genders.** A woman berating a man humiliates him, but it actually reflects very badly on both of them. A man criticising or even arguing with a woman looks like a bully.

4 **Don't project your expectations of gender roles onto others.** Stop and think about situations and behaviours in the context of the local culture. "Doing unto others as you would have them do unto you" is not always the best option when working across cultural and gender divides. You cannot assume that others want to be treated, talked to or engaged with the same way you do.

5 **Recognise the intense pressure regarding gender roles.** Your Asian contacts, friends and colleagues are likely being pulled in multiple directions simultaneously. Gender, family and professional expectations may be conflicting or even outright contradictory, and differ greatly from Western expectations. The men, for instance, have heavy responsibilities to their parents, which may influence their choices and behaviours in ways that are not always obvious.

6 **Remember that it's not your job to fix things.** You may witness examples of what to you looks like overt sexism. Your

instinct may be to get involved, to tell those present that what they are doing is wrong. This is admirable but probably not appropriate. Firstly, your views may not be aligned with either party involved. Secondly, even if you're "right", you will not be empowering anyone by "saving" them, merely reinforcing their low power position. However, if you witness physical abuse or violent exchanges, you should of course take the appropriate action.

5:
Hierarchy

"Money, status and influence are wholly interconnected in Asia. If you have one, you have the rest. You are at the top of the pyramid, and then you can do whatever you want."
— Stephen, educator, 20 years in Asia

Plymouth has always been a seafaring city. The Pilgrim Fathers set sail for America from there. Sir Francis Drake, the pirate turned privateer turned national hero, fought the Spanish Armada there. Giants of the sea were built, stationed and launched from the Dockyard – the heart of the city.

Stephen was an apprentice there, working on the commercial and naval vessels that came in for refurbishments and upgrades. He would watch them sail out of the dockyard, until they were faint dots disappearing over the horizon.

Then the world changed. The defence budgets and the ships began to go elsewhere. Whilst the unionised dockyard held out for a long time, slowly, inch by inch, it wound down and then shut down.

Stephen retrained as a teacher, and when he saw the opportunity for a job in Asia, he jumped at it. That happened 20 years ago.

Stephen sips his coffee from a "Born and bred in Devon" mug as we sit at a large wooden table under the awning outside a rather battered but clearly much-loved old house. Book-shelves line the room, and a giant stuffed marlin has pride of place across one wall. It's early in the morning and Stephen is a bit sleepy, having flown in the night before.

"I worked in a school in Thailand. The family patriarch had made money in finance and building materials. He decided on a whim to build three schools and gave them to one of his sons to run.

One day, this son was at a restaurant in town and became fascinated with watching a chef make noodles. So he paid the noodle maker to come to the school and show all the pupils how to do it. They turned up unannounced and we had to cancel all lessons so the pupils could gather to watch this guy make noodles!

Another time, he saw an old man on the street with an old-fashioned organ and dancing monkey setup. So the organ-grinder and monkey arrive at the school, and again we have to suspend all classes in the middle of the day for the kids to watch it.

Then there was the time we had the school playing field unexpectedly taken over by the owners' friends in hot-air balloons.

My favourite incident was when he came to town with his rock band. They booked a venue in a big hotel in Bangkok to play. All the school staff were instructed that they had to go. No choice. There must have been two dozen crates of Johnnie Walker stacked up behind the bar. There were bottles on every table. I have to say we actually all ended up having a really good time!

I came to realise that things work differently in Asia. Back in the UK, we have a class system, but there is a general push-back against it. If you are rich, you have a different place in society, but you are still judged the same way as everyone else and have to behave pretty much the same as everyone else. In Asia, the hierarchy is everywhere."

These examples are demonstrations of "legitimate power" – where one person has clear and acknowledged power over others, or of a situation.

Legitimate power is strongest in cultures with a high power distance index, where hierarchical structures are expected, inequalities accepted and orders unquestioned. China scores 80 on the index, India 77 and Indonesia 78. The US on the other hand scores 40, Germany and the UK both 35.

Research by the Human Capital Leadership Institute has shown that within a culture, the hierarchy (or lack of) and ways of working run smoothly because they are known and expected. The problems occur, they believe, when low-power-distance cultures and individuals interact and engage with high-power-distance colleagues and partners.

Tyson has been in Asia for 15 years, working for the giant computer software players. He wears the cargo shorts and t-shirt that are the unofficial uniform of the out-of-hours Singapore expat.

Spending time in Singapore, Malaysia and China, Tyson has learnt to be *in*, but not *of*, the local games being played. He feels strongly that that is the key to success.

"The thing to remember in Asia is that you are not in a value matrix based on quality of ideas, but one that's built around hierarchy and your role within it. If you have the right position in the hierarchy, or if people believe you are connected to or endorsed by that hierarchy, you can get an idea implemented, no matter how stupid.

When I first moved to Malaysia, I came in above a few senior people's heads. I didn't want to ruffle too many feathers, so I made every effort to integrate. To not be seen too much, or for too long, as the Western guy dropped in on them. I picked up the local vernacular, learnt the basics of the language, ate and drank with the team. I tried to assimilate. The team under and around me noticeably relaxed. Things got easier.

Then one day my boss pulled me aside. 'It's great you're trying to fit in,' he told me. 'But I didn't hire you to be local. I hired you to be a foreigner, with your foreigner's standards and demands.'

You need to balance being localised enough to understand what is going on and get things done, but remain an outsider enough to demand more – and get it."

It's easy to look at an organisational chart and think you understand the real hierarchy. You don't. Similarly, organisation size does not determine the structure or extent of the hierarchy within it, or how that company perceives its relative power compared to other players.

"Never forget the contextual nature of hierarchy. The boss is the boss is the boss. Regardless of the size of the company. If they bring five levels of seniority to a meeting, you better make sure you have five levels at that meeting. They bring the CEO? You need to have your CEO there too. Their boss wants to show they can take a strip off your team? You need someone senior enough there who will let them, to make it look real. You have to match.

I worked for the global computer and software player. We had just done a deal with a regional airline. There was going to be a press announcement in Kuala Lumpur about it. Business press, small room, podium, handshakes, the usual.

Their CEO was going to be there as the face. Fair enough, but they totally assumed that our CEO (you know who he is!) would be there too. They didn't think for a second he wouldn't be. A modestly sized regional airline CEO and the CEO of one of the world's biggest and most successful companies – to them that was parity. It took a lot of sweet talking and a few bruised egos to explain why he wouldn't be there."

Tyson is keen to step back from the specifics and make larger points about the big differences, the invisible gaps of understanding, the sheer naivety with which Westerners often approach Asia.

"I have had ideas brutally ripped to shreds in front of a roomful of people and then my next one, which was no better or worse, lavished with an embarrassing level of praise. Within 10 minutes of each other. By the same senior guy. Clearly he was making a point about something else entirely. I was his pawn.

You want to get things done? Stay close to where author-ity and influence sit. That is at the top of the hierarchy. Real power. Not titles or matrices. Who really gets thing done? Who are people scared of? Fear is a stronger motivator here than reward. Not the official lines of command, or the process, or the 'rules'. Look for the real influencers. Get close to them. It will be noted.

As the exotic foreigner with your funny ways, you will be watched constantly anyway. But how close you are to those higher up in the hierarchy – that's what people want to see. They will know how many seconds you talked to those higher up the ladder. How close you stood to them. Did they laugh? Did they back you up in front of others? If others perceive that the seniors – or even the boss – has your back on something, they will assume he is supporting everything you are doing. Then your stuff gets done.

The hierarchy is visible in other ways too. We would sometimes have parties in our apartment. Not big ones, just a few people, some music. There was someone high up living in the building – I still don't know who. At around bedtime, our electricity would suddenly get turned off. We would call every-one – the building supervisor, the power company – but no one knew anything. Then, just after our last guest left, magically the electricity would go back on."

The invisible hierarchy is just as important as the visible one. Your position in the organisation chart may indicate your official status within the pyramid, but that is only part of the evaluation. Who you have access to, how much time you spend – and are seen spending – with senior figures, your connections inside and outside of the local structure, will all impact your perceived – and real – levels of influence and access. Perception is reality. Or rather, perception can quickly become reality.

Jack has been in Asia for seven years, but he remains very English. His parents both worked for the BBC and he went to private school with the children of British rock aristocracy. He wears shiny black shoes and black socks with shorts, without irony or apology, and he rides a fold-up Brompton bicycle, a common enough sight in West London but a rarity this close to the equator.

Jack runs a company that creates materials for large construction and development projects across Asia, so he is often travelling, hopping between Bangkok, Singapore, Kuala Lumpur and Colombo. Because of the nature of the work, he engages with the very senior levels of the huge conglomerates that fund and control these multi-billion-dollar developments. This has given him a clear view of the hierarchical nature of Asian businesses, and he can see its undeniable benefits.

"The hierarchy means things can get done quickly and decisively – if you have access to the real decision-makers, that is. Without them, you are wasting your time. You can go round in circles, make everyone happy, but then when it gets to the Chairman, his is the only opinion that counts. Even if he hasn't been involved up to the point he sees it, if his comment is 'That's not what I wanted', then it's back, literally, to the drawing board.

It's not about consensus. It's the Chairman's job to know what to do. To be decisive. That's what gives people confidence. He has to have a clear point of view. He has to add value. He can't just roll along with whatever gets put in front of him.

Our teams in the UK and America provide a lot of insight and strategy as part of our service offer, either standalone or at the front end of a project. We give the client solid, well-thought-through and researched recommendations – what we, with our expertise and experience, think their course of action should be.

In Asia they often don't see the value in us doing that. Having an opinion, knowing what to do – that's the Chairman's job! He will know. Why pay a bunch of outsiders to tell them what they should think? The Chairman tells them what they should think.

It makes sense, really. Why have a guy in the top job, with the big salary, and then ask other people what should happen? He is the decision-maker. The buck stops with him. In the West we like to cover our backs. If things go wrong, then we can blame the strategy we were provided with. Absolve ourselves. In Asia the line of command and responsibility is much more clear-cut. It helps get things done."

Understanding and appreciating the dynamic of the hierarchy is working for Jack. His business is a success, and he is hiring more staff and looking to open more offices in new cities.

"You have to get a direct line to the boss. Make sure they are seeing what you are doing. Build their input into the work. Let them be the hero. Don't surprise them. Give them what they want, done really, really well."

It can go wrong, of course. When low-power-distance groups project their style and expectations onto high-power-distance cultures, teams or individuals, things can get confused. A lot of time can be wasted, discussions enter cul-de-sacs and never come out, projects stall and fail – all due to the right levels of the hierarchy not being involved at the right time and in the right ways.

Andrew, who is the regional lead for a big beer company, agrees. His job has taken him to dozens of boardrooms and hundreds of bar rooms all across Asia. He has seen the hierarchies in action on the biggest and smallest of scales.

"The issue is the pyramid nature of the organisations. You never know who the decision-maker is until you are next to them. You might be in a room with a whole bunch of people, and separately they may tell you they are in charge, that they have decision-making ability, that they can agree things with you. But are they just saying that for face? Or because they think that is what you want to hear? Maybe they don't want you to feel you have wasted your time with them? You really can't tell.

I don't know if they go away and huddle and decide between them to go to the boss or not, and what they are going to say if they do. You never see that bit. But they must be working it out somewhere. Sometimes an answer comes back. Sometimes nothing.

But then sometimes you realise you are in the room with the decision-maker. Everyone is acting differently, hanging on his every word. That's when you know you can actually get things done.

So you need to actively create those interactions. With-
out offending those lower down, you need to manufacture the
proximity to the decision-maker. You can't go over their heads
directly – that would kill the relationship with the day-to-day
team. That's bad. But you need to get close to the big guy. At
least at the start and at key points in the work."

When we are living and working in Asia, we need to identify who
has the ability to make decisions, to figure out where people
are sitting in the hierarchy. Otherwise a lot of time is spent on
those who are not able to make decisions. Building those day-
to-day relationships is vital, of course – those people are the
conduit to power – but we need to recognise when we need to
move up a level.

No one wants to admit that they cannot advance a deal,
sign off a contract or give the go-ahead on a project, particularly if they have been allowing you to hold the impression that
they can. Business in the East is full of people who don't want
to say no, but aren't empowered to say yes.

So how do you do that – go above your contact without
being seen as directing or disregarding them?

One way is to match hierarchy with hierarchy. If you want
to get access to their boss, it may mean bringing in your boss. It
is acceptable for your boss to want to see their boss. That's not
offensive. It may mean that you – and your opposite number –
won't be at that meeting, so your boss (or the individual being
presented as your boss) will need to understand what you need
from the interaction.

This is one reason formal meetings in Asia have so many
people attending. Each team member will demonstrate their

position in the hierarchy by bringing their subordinates. The other side will acknowledge the power dynamic and bring the appropriate-level team members, who will have their subordinates with them.

Lim Hwee Hua, Executive Director of Tembusu Partners, in a piece published by the Milken Institute, observed that most Asian organisations still tend to reward seniority of experience. However, these traditional seniority-based systems are quickly outliving their usefulness, in both the private and public sectors.

I'm having an early lunch with Dane on Amoy Street, just off Singapore's Central Business District. Until recently, Amoy Street was a row of small import and export businesses and traditional Chinese medicine shops. Now it bustles with restaurants, bars and co-working spaces.

Dane is good-looking, dashing in a silver fox kind of way. Not big, but perfectly proportioned, graceful and measured. Short cropped salt-and-pepper hair and a button-down shirt. Even if I didn't know, I would guess he was a very senior player in a big management consultancy. Dane doesn't ramble; he makes his points clearly and eloquently. Talking with him feels a little like having a pleasant conversation with the Harvard Business Review.

"One challenge is when local teams in Asia see Westerners come in at senior levels, or move through the ranks. It is sometimes perceived that they succeed because they are Western. In fact their success is due to the Western mindset and behaviours, because they are delivering value. Our value is in the ability to think outside of the hierarchy, to think beyond the process.

The hierarchy here exists because it needs to exist. People are more comfortable being told what to do than using their initiative and possibly doing the wrong thing. Without the hierarchy, nothing would happen.

If you want local input, you need to create a safe space, a way for thoughts to be put forward in a no-risk way. Other-wise even the whiz kids won't speak up – it is just safer to keep quiet. The fear of failure is greater than the desire for success. From an early age, the motivation is to not fail. Not really to win. But to not fail. Much better to rely on the hierarchy, the process. Don't rock it."

As we speak, the restaurant has filled up. Staff hop from table to table. Dane tries to attract our server's attention for the bill, in a good-natured way, a slight wave in her direction, a raised eyebrow as she passes. She doesn't see us.

"The problem is that this well-oiled process will only ever allow incremental growth. Breakthrough thinking is messy. It's unpre-dictable, it involves risk and potential failure. If you look at Japan, the unquestioned system of culture that delivered the successful production lines with 100% quality control resulted in huge growth. But now, that same culture is what is holding the economy back. The system can't be questioned, so break-through thinking can't happen."

As Westerners operating in Asia, we need to deliver our core tasks, do our jobs. But our key transferable skill and value is our ability to think outside of our job role. To question the process. To flag up new insights or ways of seeing things. To step outside the hierarchy.

I excuse myself from the table and go to the bathroom. Dane stays seated, trying without success to catch the eye of the server for the bill. On my way back, I pass a counter with a cash register on it and a happy staff member behind it. This is one of those places where you walk up to the counter and pay at the end. The bill doesn't come to you.

Our table server could have brought the bill perhaps, but that's not the process here. Or she could have told us about the system, but it's not her role in the hierarchy to do that either.

We should be very aware of the nature of the hierarchy that is in place, but also acknowledge that we can leverage our role as outsiders to move slightly beyond its rules, to help get things achieved. As Tyson said, "Be in it, but not of it."

Putting it into action

1 Scope out the underlying hierarchy. Before starting discussions or negotiations, try to get an understanding of where your direct contact sits in their organisation's hierarchy. Then try to find out who is empowered to make decisions. Use the organisation chart as a guide, but be aware that there will likely be hierarchies of influence within the teams and companies that are invisible. Try asking indirect questions such as "What is the sign-off process?", "Who would we need to get buy-in from?", "Is there anyone not here today that would need to see the proposals?"

② **Match hierarchy with hierarchy.** Ahead of a meeting, find out who will be present from the other team(s). Try to match their levels of hierarchy and the number of attendees. It may feel counterintuitive and inefficient to bring along "superfluous" people, but their role – displaying your understanding of and respect for the hierarchy – is in fact a vital one. After the first couple of meetings, the extras can start to be left at the office.

③ **Match boss with boss.** If a decision or buy-in is needed by someone higher up than your direct contact, you may need to bring in your bosses to move things forward. Bringing two bosses together – who until that point may have had little or nothing to do with the discussion – is a common practice. It is not a reflection on the abilities of you and your contact. Brief your boss, give them a clear understanding of the work done so far, and what you need them to achieve. Your counterpart should be doing the same. It is possible you will not even be at the bosses' meeting – that's fine. With agreement, or the right approvals given, you can then continue taking the project forward.

④ **Stay positive when blocked by hierarchical barriers.** No matter how well you structure a proposal or solution with your direct contact, the final decision may be made by someone higher up the hierarchy whom you have not met, in a meeting you will not attend. Do your best to help whoever will be at that meeting be prepared with all the salient points, arguments, facts and figures. Also, ensure the decision-maker is given your contact details, and make yourself available to answer any questions they have, remotely, during the session.

⑤ **Make use of wiggle room within the hierarchy.** As a relative outsider, you may be able to talk to those one (or even two) levels above or below you in the hierarchy. Just ensure you are not discussing points that should be made with your opposite number or through the correct channels. You may be able to suggest ways of moving a project forward outside of the usual process, and you can ask "dumb" questions that allow parties to relook working processes in a non-threatening way.

⑥ **Make use of your "privileged" position – judiciously.** Within global organisations, there is often an international hierarchy that the local hierarchy may operate wholly or partly within. You may be perceived as being part of that larger, separate hierarchy, with connections to decision-makers and influencers outside the local sphere. This in itself may grant you access to people on the ground locally that you would not normally have access to. Equally, you may find people higher up the pyramid approaching and engaging you, in order to gain access to your international network. Use this special privilege wisely, and remember these favours and access will likely have to be reciprocated later.

⑦ **Put aside your personal feelings on hierarchy.** You may feel more comfortable with a low-power style and encourage others to feel and act the same way. You may feel that a hierarchical structure and the associated behaviours are counter-productive to team building and delivery of results. You may feel that people delver their best work in open, flat structures. You may be right. But that is irrelevant. The hierarchy exists. It is the system that people know and are comfortable with. Open-ended questions, ambiguous instructions, vague process – to Westerners these may be empowering; to Asians it is likely confusing. Bring your style to the table, of course, but don't expect to single-handedly change thousands of years of social conditioning with an open-door policy, casual Fridays and beanbags in the meeting room.

6:
Standing Out

"The fat pig gets eaten first."
— Simon, broadcaster and
businessman, 20 years in Asia

In China, there is an expression, "The fat pig gets eaten first". For a family get-together or the New Year, the farmer goes down to the pig pen to choose dinner. Which of his pigs does he choose? The quiet, little one in the background, or the big, confident one that sticks its head up and says, "Look at me"? He kills the fat pig. They roast the fat pig. They eat the fat pig.

What the phrase means is, keep your head down, keep quiet. People will go after the most obvious target, so don't do anything that will make you stand out.

Whilst in the West we nurture and encourage individuality, uniqueness and standing out from the crowd, in Asia it is frowned upon. As we have discussed in other chapters, in Asia the group is often seen as more important than the individual, and saving face and avoiding risk are key behavioural drivers. This combination of influences and considerations results in a population that is often very reluctant to stand out from the crowd or become more visible than is necessary.

This feeling can be summed up in a single Japanese word, *yokonarabi*. It literally translates as "to line up sideways". Better to keep in line with others (even when they are the competition) than to stand out ahead of them.

In a situation where a Westerner sees a chance to display their individuality, their intelligence, their wit or their opinions, an Asian will see the risk of looking arrogant, acting rude, sounding foolish or being wrong. If a question thrown out to a lecture theatre remains unanswered, it is not that the students don't understand it, or have a different opinion or a question to ask. It's because it would be bad form, and risky, to speak up. Same opportunity, but totally different views on the potential outcomes.

Researchers Heejung Kim and Hazel Rose Marcus spent a day in an international airport and asked a mix of American, European and Asian volunteers to take a short test. As a reward for completing the test, the participants were given a pen as a gift. They were shown four pens, and asked to choose one for themselves. This was the real test.

Three of the pens were the same, while the fourth one was different. Which pen do you think the volunteers chose?

The Westerners chose the single different pen, the one-off. The Asians chose one of the three "majority" pens. With these choices, the Americans and Europeans overwhelmingly demonstrated their desire for distinction and independence by selecting the unique option. The Asians did the exact opposite.

What's interesting is that these volunteers made their choices knowing quite well that no one else would ever know if they had chosen a unique pen or a common pen; they would just see a single pen. Even though their choice to be individual or play it safe would be invisible to others, it still dictated their decision. That's how deeply rooted the instinct to stand out – or not stand out – is.

Another experiment looked beyond the individual and into the wider fabric of society and culture. Researchers analysed nearly 300 full-page magazine advertisements in America and Korea. They coded the content of these ads and divided them into those that featured individualism, self-determining behaviours and uniqueness (e.g. words such as "freedom", "possibilities", "choose your own view") versus those that referenced the group, society and conformity (e.g. terms such as "tradition" and "home", and phrases like "7 out of 10 people" which offer the chance to be part of a bigger group).

What did they find? 95% of the Korean ads had some kind of conformity theme, while 89% of the US ads had a uniqueness theme.

Advertising is a very, very expensive business. The high investment level means that a lot of time, money and effort is put into tracking the results and ensuring the works' effectiveness. There are a number of incredibly complex and robust metrics in place. Tracking and analysing advertising effectiveness is an industry in itself.

If Korean ads are predominantly focusing on the group and conformity to sell a product or service, then that is because that approach has been demonstrated beyond reasonable doubt to work. The same for the US ads. If they are consistently featuring uniqueness and individuality, then that's because that is what has been proven to turn readers into consumers!

Conformity and individualism do more than influence the behaviours of individuals. The pursuit of them dictates product choices, which in turn drives whole industries.

I'm talking to Jen. She works in advertising and has spent five years in Asia. As we talk, the band starts to play the opening chords of "Hotel California". Families sit on blankets on the sports field in front of the stage. Fathers and sons throw footballs back and forth to each other, whilst their families eat hotdogs and ribs, washed down with beer and soda. Small and large American flags, hanging from every available point, flutter in the light breeze. It is the Fourth of July weekend.

Jen's enthusiasm for life, her confidence, her New World energy fit the surroundings perfectly.

"I was working for one of the big global ad agencies. We did a large training session here in Asia. Mostly Asians attending, and a couple of Americans. All the trainers were American.

I now know that Asians don't speak up in a group environment. It makes them feel uncomfortable and they don't feel it is necessary. They certainly don't want to shout out answers on topics they don't know much about in front of a room full of strangers. Americans, heck, we love a chance to show how smart we are, shouting out answers, coming up with ideas.

But clearly the trainers had no idea of the Asian perspective. No idea at all. They would make a point on a topic, then throw out a question to the room and wait for an answer. Then they would wait. And wait. And wait. Till it became really awkward. They just didn't get that most of the room didn't want to speak up. So they would start badgering them. Still nothing. Just even more awkward."

Jen takes a bite of her hotdog and makes a sweeping gesture over the crowd.

"It's not like there is a right or wrong. Just different. The trainers should have known that. They should have put in mechanics to allow the groups to ask questions in a different format. Small groups. One-to-ones. Whatever. But they didn't. So the awkward silences continued.

Eventually, just to break the stalemate, I answered. So we could move on. Next question. Silence again, and again, eventually I answered. Then a third time. Then, as if it couldn't get any worse, another American shouted out, 'Don't worry, everyone. The Americans will answer all the questions for you!'"

Children push past us, and as the band moves on to Bruce Springsteen, Jen continues:

"It's not isolated. I've seen this or something similar repeated time and time again across the region, by people that don't bother to think that there might be an alternative to their way of thinking, working and acting.

If we want to work well together, to integrate, to get the best out of each other, we have to stop being provincial in our thinking."

Jen is right. It is hard to truly understand the wider context, or the people in it, when you refuse or are unable to get out of the bubble you came in. We need to break out of our preconceived expectations and comfort zone. Step into the actual world we are inhabiting, not the one we brought with us.

But I have to admit, sometimes it is tempting and all too easy to stay in that bubble. My meeting with Jen, the band, the hotdogs, the flags, all took place in the grounds of an American school... in Singapore.

In Asia, these primary behavioural differences can be visible in experiences that we believe are truly global. Let's go to Disneyland.

Disneyland Tokyo looks very much like a Disneyland in the US. Castles, cartoon characters, princesses, nausea-inducing rides, and thousands and thousands of families. Grown-ups and kids walk through the park together, holding hands, riding on shoulders, expectantly looking to see what wonder is around the next corner. It's almost exactly the same as in the US, except for one big difference.

It's quiet.

At first glance, you could be excused for thinking the attendees at Disneyland Tokyo don't enjoy visiting the park, that they aren't having fun. But that's not the case. The incredibly high attendance figures and return rates are proof of that.

In their book *Clash!*, Hazel Rose Markus and Alana Conner believe that the screams, whoops, exclamations you hear in the US, compared to the silence of the Asian parks, are indications of behavioural norms, not an indication of how much people are enjoying themselves. The Tokyo visitors are having great fun, they just aren't making a lot of fuss about it.

Markus and Conner believe that in Asia, people want to be aware of their feelings so that they can be sure they are displaying the right one, and in the right amount. They want to be suitably happy within the parameters of acceptable display; then they can relax and enjoy the experience.

The desire to blend in goes beyond the actions of the individual. It can also be seen in a number of other outward social projections. Style of dress is usually muted, cars will most often not be adorned with personal touches, grand homes may often be hidden behind humble facades

Bob, a global creative director (who we hear more from in the chapter about Relationships), gives an example of this:

"Quite early in my years in Moscow, I remember going to visit a couple of friends of mine at their apartment. They were a rather successful business couple I had met through some mutual friends.

The taxi to their apartment building went through a complex series of alleys, and finally dropped me off in a location that I had to assume was a mistake. To my Western eyes the building looked like a wreck. Peeling paint, overgrown garden, and what looked like extremely suspect plumbing and wiring. It looked like it was in a Demilitarised Zone. I even questioned the cab driver as to whether he had made some sort of mistake. He assured me it was the right location.

I pressed the intercom buzzer and heard my friend's voice. 'Come on up!' I entered the building and began to climb a set of dilapidated stairs past a set of broken mailboxes. I came to their apartment door (which looked fortified) and was greeted by my friend.

As I stepped inside, the transition could not have been more remarkable. Their apartment was a haven of bright, modern interior design, beautifully decorated and full of every possible mod con.

Over dinner, I asked about the contrast and got a little Russian life lesson. For Russians, the focus is always on what they can control – the things that matter to them. Those were internal things. And the exterior of their building was no one's priority. Their community came together to fix what needed fixing, but for the most part, each family's focus was on their own personal space.

In Russia, you can't judge anything by what you see on the surface. It's all about what's inside.

You can see it play out in what people identify with, what they aspire to. You can see how something that works for a brand in the West wholly misses the mark in other geographies. In the West, we value independence, men of action, going out on your own, making your own path, knowing you did it your way, standing out from the herd. This is more important than aligning with others. None of this is true in Asia. Status, blending in, being part of the group – those are important.

Do you want an example? The Marlboro Man. Rugged. Independent. Proud. Stands alone. Stands out from the crowd. That image, that man, turned around the fortunes of the Marlboro brand. Their whole positioning, all their success, was built on men wanting to be that man.

We tested it in China. Their reaction: 'That poor farmer can't even afford a tractor.'

Completely different! No one wants to be that guy. He's a loser. Out on his own. No family. No friends. Nothing to show for his life. Why would anyone want to be that? Same cowboy, polar opposite reactions."

As a Westerner, your inclination may be to promote yourself and pursue actions that help you to stand out, to raise yourself out from the crowd, to push yourself forward. These actions may be a little risky, or may not be for the overall benefit of the team, the group, or the nation, but as you are the driving force and you are the star of your own movie, you do them.

This is so deeply rooted in our thinking that most of us are not even aware that it is a choice we are making. However, we need to remain highly aware of the fact that the behaviours we value and expect are not universally shared. Others will likely have very different priorities and preferred scenarios.

If we are unaware of these differences, problems can arise where in fact there are none. We may perceive conflict where none exists. Underlying agreement can be clouded by surface differences in emotional style.

Ray heads a scientific research team at a highly prestig-ious institution in Singapore. His work is known globally and his professional reputation is one of highly credible authority, based on years of diligent work and solid results. But Ray does not look like the scientist of popular culture. There is no mop of messy white hair, no paunch or hunch, no exaggerated arm waving or forehead slapping. Ray looks to be in his mid-30s but I know he is a decade older than that. He has neatly cropped brown hair. He is physically well-toned and conveys a love of life and his discipline. When we meet, he has just come from the gym.

"Whenever I was teaching or with the members of my research team, I would never get asked direct questions. But then, after I left the lecture or the lab, by the time I got into a cab, there

would be a flood of emails. All asking, very politely, questions it would have been a lot easier to ask me – and for me to answer – five minutes earlier.

I realised I needed to create a safe space for the questions. Now, before I finish a lecture or leave the lab for the day, I say, 'I'm going to sit here for five minutes, with nothing else to do. If anyone has any questions, just come over and ask me one-to-one.'

Removing the public aspect of asking questions removes one of the key barriers. Now I have people lining up to talk to me! You need to create a bridge to independent thought. People are watched by their families like hawks to ensure they stay in the success lane. You don't drift out of the lane by thinking for yourself! The family structure perpetuates this.

My PhD students and junior team members will usually still live at home. They don't make many of the decisions that Westerners in the same position – but living independently – would. Where to live, what to eat, how to behave... these are still being set by the family. This absence of physical and social independence directly affects the ability to be intellectually independent or confident. This, then, reinforces the desire to fit in, stay within the rules, stick to one's lane, and not stand out.

Funnily, some of my students became clones of me. In an effort not to stand out, they decided to emulate my style, mannerisms and habits. It is safer to try and blend in by being a safe figure, rather than risk standing out as an individual. It is less exposure to be a copy of the professor! That removes one dangerous variable."

Putting it into action

(1) Conduct discussions in smaller groups. One-to-one or one-to-two settings work well. It may be counterintuitive, but it is often more productive to have a series of small meetings than a single large one. If you need to plan a group interaction, keep it as small as possible and try to avoid asking for comments or questions from a group of over three or four people. When a large group is unavoidable, let people know that you will be available for one-to-one or smaller group discussions afterward.

(2) Avoid questions that put people on the spot. Circumstances may make it necessary to ask questions directly to people publicly. If so, offer a choice of options or answers, rather than proposing open-ended questions. A question that can be adequately answered with a yes or no is more likely to get a response than a "What do you think?", "What are your thoughts on...?" or "How do you feel about....?"

(3) Read between the lines of the silent response. If you ask a direct question to an individual and the response is silence, this doesn't mean they're ignoring you or didn't hear the question. Smiling or even laughing is not a sign of disrespect. These reactions could all stem from awkwardness or possibly fear of saying the wrong thing. Try rephrasing the question in a more straightforward way. Make it clear that "I don't know" is an acceptable response. If the silence becomes too awkward, simply say something along the lines of "No problem – if we can't answer that now, we can return to it later" and move on.

④ **Compliment people on displays of independence of thought or courage.** Not acknowledging when someone has taken a risk by putting forward an idea misses an important opportunity to build trust. Never dismiss or reject a comment put forward, whether as an unconsidered reaction or as a deliberate strategy to prove someone wrong or to display your superior knowledge. It will shut down any further input from not just that individual, but likely everyone else present.

⑤ **Remember that imitation is the sincerest form of flattery.** It is also a survival instinct. You may see your mannerisms, habits, modes of speech being copied. This is not mockery. You may see chunks of your thinking repackaged and represented. This is not dishonesty. To a more junior, risk-averse individual, aligning themselves with a successful or senior figure's style or thinking is a safe bet.

⑥ **Don't judge an individual's ability based on their appetite for the spotlight.** Risk and opportunity are flip sides of the coin. Where Westerners may see in an opportunity the chance to display their talents, Asians may see in that same opportunity the risk of exposing their weaknesses. Regardless of the skills of the individuals, they may choose to seize it, or shy away from it. It is foolish to attempt to gauge the skills, intelligence, confidence or talents of the individuals based on their decision to embrace or shun the spotlight.

7:
Character

"In Asia, the character
of the person is more
important than the
quality of the idea."
— Jay, serial entrepreneur,
15 years in Asia

Confucian teaching emphasises the importance of having – and nurturing – the right character traits. Confucius believed we are all born with innately good character, but over time it is our choice as to whether we develop the better aspects of our character through education, self-reflection and personal cultivation – or succumb to the baser elements of our character.

"Ye shall know them by their fruits," says the King James Bible. In other words, you know a person by what they produce, the visible manifestation of what is going on within.

On the other hand, the Buddha says, "Peace comes from within. Do not seek it without." What is happening inside is what truly counts; what happens outside is the just visible aspect of that.

This is a deeply rooted divergence – how we differently prioritise and value character and action.

Jay is a successful entrepreneur. He has founded startups in Silicon Valley, London, Kenya and Singapore. Jay is soft-spoken, with dazzlingly active eyes. He has dark, well-kept hair and a light complexion. Not Caucasian, not Indian, not really Southeast Asian. It would be impossible to make a confident guess at Jay's ethnicity. Jay is one of the few truly global citizens I have ever met. He has seen first-hand the relative importance of character versus idea in the decision-making of investors and venture capitalists around the world.

"In Silicon Valley, the idea is the main thing. The founder can be a total jerk, but if he has got a good idea, an idea that people believe in, he can get the backing. Sometimes it seems that the more of an arrogant jerk the founder is, the more likely he is to get backing! That self-belief is magnetic. VCs will often back up a jerk with a team of their choosing – people that will balance out the jerk's flaws and act as a buffer."

In Asia, it is 100% the other way around. The character of the founder is what investors are evaluating. What kind of person is he? Is he honourable? Can I trust him? Will he work hard? Can I introduce him to my contacts without fear of being embarrassed?

"In Asia, people wouldn't see the logic of hiring or backing someone of poor character and then working around them. They would want someone of good character, then help develop them even further. Being an arrogant jerk may work

sometimes in the West, but that is no reason to think it will ever work elsewhere."

Humility and the desire to self-improve are powerful and sought-after character traits in Asia. This hypothesis has been put to the test by a number of academic research projects. A study by M.R. Lepper and D. Greene in the *Journal of Personality and Social Psychology* perfectly makes the point.

In the study, Canadian and Japanese student volunteers took a pen-and-paper test. They were not told about the real reason for the test or the nature of the experiment.

Half the participants were given an easy test that they were likely to do well on; the other half were given a much more difficult test, which they were likely to struggle with. After the test was taken, the students were given the answers and graded themselves. Predictably, some did as well as or better than they expected and some did worse.

They were then asked to wait for the second part of the test to start, which was on a computer. The facilitator at this point pretended to be unable to operate the equipment and went to seek the help of a colleague. Whilst waiting, the students were told that they could take another test, like the previous pen-and-paper one, if they wanted. Taking this additional test was optional and wouldn't affect the results of the overall testing.

The Canadians that had done well on the original test were much more likely to start the additional one than those that had done poorly; and once they started, they persisted with it longer. They knew they were good at it, so wanted to do it more.

On the other hand, the Japanese that had done *badly* on the original test were more likely to take the second one and stick at it longer than those that had done well. The ones that had done badly wanted to go back and try it again, to get better.

If you are Canadian, you will likely avoid what you are bad at, and keep doing what you are good at. If you are Japanese, you will quickly put a mental tick next to what you are good at, and keep going back to what you are poor at.

Another experiment – featured in Hazel Rose Markus and Alana Conner's *Clash!* – showed that not only do Asians see themselves as being affected by the wider context, they also tend to place themselves squarely in the middle of that context. Never near the edges. Better to be underestimated, even by yourself, than to dangerously stand out.

In this study, students were asked to estimate what percentage of the class they thought was smarter than them. The American students on average estimated 30%; they thought they were smarter than 70% of the class. The Japanese on average estimated 50%; they put themselves right in the middle of the class.

Markus and Conner point out that it might be tempting from a Western viewpoint to think that the Japanese were an unhappy bunch. That they felt inferior and did not have the self-confidence of the Americans.

But the opposite seems to be true. Depression levels are lower in Japan than in the US. Perhaps having a more realistic viewpoint and slightly underestimating yourself prevents disappointment. Having a lower opinion of yourself and therefore expectations of what you can achieve means you will be more satisfied with how your life turns out.

My conversation with Jay continues from character to behaviour. Bad behaviour when away from home may be a universal character flaw, but for the purposes of this book we will look at the impact of Western behaviour on the perception of their character by Asian colleagues, contacts and peers.

"You often see Westerners do things whilst in Asia that they would never do back home. They may be rude and thoughtless. They may visit strip joints, girlie bars, massage parlours. They may get drunk and loud. It is almost as though how your character may be perceived here is less important than in the West. As though what people think of you matters less here. In fact it is exactly the opposite!"

As Westerners, we may attribute this to a "When in Rome" or "What happens on tour, stays on tour" mentality, and make excuses for it.

To the Asian observer, however, this sort of behaviour may communicate several possible messages:

1: You think so little of your host's country and culture that you feel you can behave any way you want and not bother about the consequences.
2: This kind of behaviour is normal for you, and you do it all the time, everywhere.
3: You are the kind of person that always wants to do these things, but you lack the guts do it at home, and can only do it "anonymously" in another part of the world.

Which of these do you want thought of you? Hopefully none.

There is a saying, "A weak man cannot be virtuous". In Asia it is often pointed out that lack of opportunity is not the same as strength of character. Not doing something because you do not have the chance to do so (bully, cheat, be unfaithful, etc) is not the same as not doing it because you believe it is wrong. That is why it is not uncommon for a Westerner to be given the opportunity to display their true character by their Asian hosts, contacts or colleagues.

I recall a situation in Cambodia. I was at a KTV bar with a potential client. At about 1 am, the call girls were brought into the room and I was asked which one I wanted to take to the hotel. It was incredible pressure. A dozen Cambodian guys shouting encouragement and suggestions, whilst their boss, the CEO, my potential client, looked on.

The women had numbers on their wrists, like beauty pageant contestants. We'd all been singing karaoke and drinking whisky. A lot of whisky. I knew what they wanted me to do. What would no doubt win us the pitch. But fundamentally that is not the kind of person I am.

It had taken months to get this far. The old saying, "Ten meetings to money" – meaning it takes a long time to build a relationship in Asia before business can even begin – was almost spot-on in this case. We'd had phone conversations, coffee, credentials meetings, follow-up meetings, initial presentations, drinks together. They kept talking about wanting a long-term partner, not just an agency. They didn't seem to be in any kind of rush. It made us hopeful.

So, now we'd been pitching all afternoon, against another team, who'd been allowed to stay and watch us. We were working through a translator, who I later found out we didn't really need, as the CEO and his team all spoke English, but who was there for protocol.

They seemed to like what they saw and as we went for dinner and then drinks after, they started talking about giving us a special treat later. It got less subtle as the night wore on. When I realised what they were talking about over dinner, I tried to make it clear that it wasn't my thing. That I was married. That I wasn't interested. I repeated the point in the bar. But after the singing, out came the girls.

I didn't cave in. Despite the pressure, the encouragement, the insinuations. Eventually they got bored of me and turned to the guy from the other agency. He tried to decline, for a while, but then gave in. The crowd cheered his decision. I went back to my hotel knowing I had lost us the job.

Then after a week or so passed, we got a call. We had won the job. I was baffled. The official brief came to us, the budget was agreed and we started work. A couple of months later, the CEO's younger brother – I think his title was CMO – flew in to review the first stages of work. I asked him about it over a beer.

It turns out the CEO didn't really care if I went with a girl or not. He was interested in what sort of man I was. He wanted to see if I would stick to my guns, or cave in under pressure after a few drinks.

What I did in the moment was only important in how it related to who I was. Had I shown myself to be of good character? Had I stayed true to what I had said previously? Did they feel I was the kind of person that they could have a long-term relationship with? And the answer was yes. I definitely didn't see that coming.

High-context cultures (Asia) look at the impact of an individual's character on the group, on the cooperation and collaboration between people, in order to achieve larger – often longer-term – results that benefit a large number of people. Asian cultures are orientated around family, geography, business or country; these priorities are reflected in the desired character traits that an individual will hold and display. In these cultures, the person whose character supports the "We" is most valued.

In low-context cultures (the West), focus is on the individual. On personal effort and often short-term achievements. We look at individual responsibility and reward. We are competitive, even with others in our families or businesses (whom we should probably work better with!). In these cultures, the character traits that most support and promote the "I" are most valued.

Research into the importance of character in Asia is surprisingly slim, but as a subject it is sometimes referred to as virtue ethics.

Virtue ethics is evaluating an individual not by their actions but by who they are as a person. It is concerned with the inner character and moral virtue of the person, not any of their specific actions. Virtue ethics is not interested in the right or wrong of a specific action. Actions are perhaps only able to reflect the moral virtue of a person if viewed in the totality of their life.

So a man of good character will, through his actions, do the right thing, and in doing so, positively impact others. Character informs action. If someone has good character, you can be pretty sure that their actions will be good. So the belief goes.

Existing research has highlighted the admired character traits of successful and well-known leaders in the West and in Asia.

In the West, we look up to figures like Steve Jobs and Jack Welch. They are seen as decisive, visionary, sure-footed. They are proud, they are bold and they are action-orientated. But in Asia, the research conducted by Burak Oc (Bocconi University), Gary Greguras (Singapore Management University), Michael Bashshur (Singapore Management University), and James Diefendorff (Akron University) has shown that most CEOs value attributes that are deeper, cultivated and less immediately visible.

The values and character traits identified as most valuable by the Asian CEOs were notably benevolence, harmony, learning, loyalty, righteousness and humility. These are core Confucian doctrines.

The research summarised what the respondents believed were the key aspects of good character:

1: Knowing who you are (and being OK with it)
2: Recognising the strengths and achievements of others
3: Listening to input from others and being teachable
4: Leading by example
5: Being humble, avoiding arrogance and letting others shine
6: Having empathy for others
7: Showing respect to others and being fair
8: Helping to develop others

This clearly highlights the distinction between character and action, which lies at the core of possibly the most commonly seen divergence between East and West. The West values what you do; Asia values who you are.

This focus on learning, humility and self-development is deeply embedded – from the first day of school. Western schools champion individual attributes, the belief that each person can achieve anything they set out to do; that we stand and fall on our individual skills and grit. Motivation is toward excelling and being seen as a singular talent.

In Asian schools, on the other hand, the emphasis is on the repeated practice and mastering of core skills. Of protocols between students and teachers. Of respect and understanding of acceptable behaviours. Motivation is built on avoiding falling behind, not dropping low in class, not being sub-par.

But do not for a second think that avoiding "failure" is easier than striving after success. Like the nuclear arms race, the level of commitment required just to stay at the table goes up and up continuously. Asian children will very often be attending 10–20 hours of after-school supplementary classes per week. As a Westerner, it is hard to imagine the pressure levels.

In the West, we believe in the primacy of the individual. The entrepreneur, the rebel, the tortured artist, the lonely genius. One person against the world. Cutting their own path against the odds. The rule-breaker, the game-changer. The Asian mindset is not the same. In Asia, the group is paramount. The family, the business, the nation. Hard work and endeavour is valued – in fact is often expected much more than in the West – but it is directed toward the common good. It builds. It adds value to the whole. The West's notion of valuable disruption and necessary conflict is alien. Harmony, humility and self-improvement are key in most things.

Before entering into a relationship – whether giving you a job, bringing you onto a team or awarding a project – the Asian standpoint is to find out who you are. Who you really are. Deep, deep down. That is what will inform the decision.

Putting it into action

1 **Watch your character in every interaction – even "minor" ones.** You will be evaluated not just by what you can deliver on the day or how you conduct yourself with the CEO, but how you act every day. Take care in every interaction, particularly those which you may not feel have any real implication. How you talk to the waiter, whether you tip, if you offer to assist in a menial task, how you engage with the receptionist, your punctuality and your displays of honesty, are all important. In Asian cultures, these interactions combine to form the assessment of your character.

2 **Be humble.** In Asia, humility in a Westerner is viewed as a kind of superpower! Humility, modesty and the primacy of the group are character traits highly valued in Asia. In the West, on the other hand, confidence, individuality and the drive to deliver change are most valued. Be honest with yourself as to where your natural inclination lies, and try to open up some space to nurture other traits. The best answer, as usual, is somewhere between the extremes.

3 **Guard the integrity of your character wherever you are.** Your character is not situation-dependent, so it should not vary at different times or in different places. If a behaviour or action would be out of character for you in one place (e.g. at home), then you shouldn't do it in any place (while "on tour"). In an Asian context, it reflects a weakness of character.

4 **Do not give in to peer pressure.** This may come from Western colleagues or Asian hosts. Identify what your boundaries and personal rules are, and stick to them. Ask yourself what you feel is the right thing to do – that is following your character. Peer validation is fleeting, but reputation and the effect of "displays of character" last for years.

5 **Remember that the character traits we value are culturally specific.** Do not turn your inclinations into expectations of others. You may value drive, ambition and a "get things done no matter what" attitude, but those may not be the traits desired by other cultures or individuals. Others with different character strengths are not "less good at being you"; they are very good at being them.

6 **Don't expect the group to adjust to you.** In the West, a talented individual may expect a team to morph around them to compensate for their weaker areas. Their strengths are worth putting up with their weaknesses for. That is often not the case in Asia. No matter how smart you are, or how great your idea is, bad character or behaviour will not be tolerated. In the West we are starting to embrace the idea of the "No Asshole Rule". In Asia it has always been so.

8:
Time Perception

"In the West, we
think in terms of financial
quarters. In Asia, they think
in terms of human history."
— Ambassador Karsten Warnecke

Karsten is the Executive Director of the Asia-Europe Foundation (ASEF), an organisation set up to promote and facilitate
interaction and understanding between Asia and Europe.

*"For thousands of years, Asia and the West interacted. We
traded goods and information. But there was only a handful of
people actually in contact from one side to the other. They were
experts in it. Their families had probably been playing that role
for generations. It was very contained. But now, the volume of
interaction is unprecedented."*

We are sitting at a high table outside a bar on a busy street.
There are no walls to the sides of the bar, so the street and the

bar blend into each other. As buses drive by, we momentarily pause our conversation. In a corner the cricket is playing on a large TV screen.

Karsten is measured and highly articulate. He speaks without hesitation and with a quiet confidence. You get the feeling he is not often contradicted, particularly on this subject. With close-cropped grey hair, sparkling eyes and a tiny stud in his left earlobe, he looks like a successful German diplomat. Which he is.

"Historically, even when people were interacting for the first time across Asia and the West, the time taken to travel from place to place meant the change was slow. There were gradual geographic and climate shifts. You would see the world, the people, the culture change gradually as you went through them. You had time to adapt.

Now you can get on a plane in Germany and a few hours later you land in Beijing, or New Delhi, or Jakarta. There is no time to adjust, to learn, to adapt. You are thrust into a new landscape.

Plus, the nature of trade, until recently, was always complementary. Asia had things the West didn't have but wanted, and were happy to pay or trade for. The West had things Asia didn't, and they were happy to trade for those. It was a win-win, each side giving the other something they wanted and that they could take back to their geography and profit from.

But when both sides want the same thing from each other, or both sides have the same thing to sell, then it immediately becomes competitive. That's when the tension, the games and the conflict start.

The Chinese think long-term. We think more about quar-terly financial results. They are thinking generations ahead. In Europe, we think problem-solution-problem-solution in a constant tactical churn. In China, they aren't thinking about skirmishes or individual battles.

Sometimes it will even seem as though the Chinese act against their own interests. That decisions being made are detrimental to their political influence or economic well-being. To our eyes this is puzzling. We don't see that these aren't decisions made for short-term gain, but as part of achieving a much longer-term victory."

Time is relative. Different cultures may not experience time faster or slower, but they certainly have a different attitude toward it. Of course, individuals within a culture will differ in their relationships with time – some will be laidback, some sticklers for punctuality – but overall we can place cultures on a spectrum.

Edward Hall (*The Silent Language*) saw cultures' relation-ship to time as either monochronic or polychronic.

Monochronic cultures see time as simple, consistent and linear. It is constantly moving forward. This is the West. Poly-chronic cultures see time as layered, fluid and cyclical. It ebbs and flows. This is Asia.

In the West, we are obsessed with tracking time. We have clocks on our walls, on our wrists, on our phones, and ticking away in the top corner of our computer screens. Things start and stop punctually at regular and prearranged times, and pro-fessionals bill their time in hours (or minutes!). Businesses are assessed primarily on their performance that financial quarter.

"Time waits for no man" and "Time is money", we are told, so we divide time up further and further.

Because our time is a commodity that is closely rationed, tracked, bought and sold, we naturally evaluate situations and people based on what we see and hear in a very tight chronological window. What just happened? What is about to happen? What was the quality or result of the last thing that was delivered?

Bob, a global creative director (who we meet properly in the chapter on Relationships), and I were sitting outside a restaurant near the river in Melbourne, when he talked insightfully on the subject.

Russia, Bob asserts – and the research backs him up – is an Asian country. Its family focus, emphasis on strong friendship bonds, the importance of honour and face, and in particular the relationship with time, make it clearly a high-context culture. The reticence Westerners have about identifying Russia as an Asian country is simply due to the fact that most Russians don't look stereotypically Asian. We are guilty of projecting our Western values and expectations onto Russians simply because we think they look Western.

"When I first moved to Moscow, I was sent to help turn around a department that was seen as underperforming by the global HQ of our company. Having a pretty strong record in this type of role, I confidently felt I would be looking at a timeline of six months to turn things around. How wrong I was.

Like relationships, timelines in business in Russia are based on commitment and time. Before people will follow you, they genuinely need to trust you. And this simply takes time and consistent actions. One of my most senior people, and eventually one of my strongest team members, was initially so hesitant to work with me that she went on leave. It took over 12 months simply to convince her to get back onboard.

The truth is, it took me those first six months to understand the level of patience and commitment the turnaround would require. And in fact the entire process to get the organisation aligned and onboard was a three-year exercise!

Business in Russia requires an understanding of the slooooooooow burn. Not so much tortoise and hare but tortoise and slightly slower tortoise! You need patience. You have to be consistent."

In the West, we see time and activity as sequential. We do one thing at a time, and one thing leads to another. Time is seen as the conduit for basic cause and effect. We like advance planning, we like to get to the point, and we usually want to know what is going to happen next.

In the East, time is less of a measured commodity. It is seen in a much, much larger and wider context. So conversations and meetings may meander, people may wander off-topic, others may chip in and take the lead for a while. The activity of the discussion itself may seem more important than the destination – which to us would be a long-awaited conclusion.

In the West, we will usually see a deadline as a hard-and-fast point in time. We generally believe that deadlines are to be hit, unless there is a very good reason. In the East, deadlines are often seen more as a target, something to be aimed for, but not set in stone. If circumstances change, priorities shift, then the timeline will change accordingly.

From an objective point of view, the Asian mindset is more logical than the Western one. Outside factors, priorities or influences may change, so we should adjust ambitions and expectations accordingly. But for Westerners this fluidity can be confusing and frustrating. We fear that one shifting fluid deadline will knock onto our other (seemingly) more rigid ones.

Personally, working in India fundamentally changed my perception of time. Even before I went there, it was already changing how I looked at things. Getting my first India visa in London was an ordeal. Queuing up for hours only to discover I was in the wrong queue, or that I needed a piece of paperwork from a different queue before I could proceed at this one. Counter staff listened to my requests and then just got up and walked away.

I remember getting to the final stage (I thought) and moving into the final waiting room. There were maybe 200 people in there. The chairs were bolted to the floor. One wall was made up of counters. Most were unmanned. Kids were running around, people wandering in different directions. I held my little pink number ticket, sat down and stared intently up at the ticket number screen. My number was a lot higher than the one showing! After 10 minutes the number hadn't changed. I realised I was going to be there for a long time and I started to feel stressed.

Sitting next to me was an old Indian man who had a tiffin box, a flask, a cushion, a paperback book and a newspaper. Amid the chaos, he looked totally calm. He looked at me, smiled, and said, "India starts here."

When I returned next time, I took snacks, a book and wore more comfortable clothes!

When in Asia, the combination of people's more relaxed attitude to punctuality and the strict hierarchies can be very frustrating. Firstly, things won't start on time, so don't expect them to. A meeting in the morning will start late; this will knock on the next meeting, which will start late, and may be interrupted part-way through, so will overrun even more. By the time you get to late afternoon, each meeting (and people love to have meetings) started and finished later and later than planned. The final meeting might start a couple of hours late – or, if it is near or past the end of the day, be cancelled.

The more rigid hierarchy means you may be dumped in reaction to a demand from higher up the hierarchy. You may be sitting in the lobby waiting for a meeting to start, but if your contact has been summoned by his boss, or suddenly needs to deliver something for a senior figure, you will be told the meeting will start late and be asked to wait. The wait could be long, and could still result in you eventually being told the meeting has been cancelled.

I have had clients receive calls part-way through a one-to-one presentation or meeting, and they have just excused themselves, got up and left the room. On one occasion, I was left sitting alone in the room for around 30 minutes before the client returned. On another occasion, I waited for around 10 minutes, and then his assistant came in to tell me he would not be returning and we would need to reschedule.

This behaviour is not being rude; and when subjected to it, you are not being treated discourteously. People are just working within their set of norms, abiding by how things work in their culture. They know that other people would – and do – do it to them all the time.

My longest wait was seven hours, to meet the Chairman of a big Indian corporation to present some final-stage work. They had a big presence at an event they were sponsoring. The big boss was somewhere there and I was asked to wait in the "hospitality" tent. It was a large, bare canvas structure with plywood floors. It was very hot and the acts were practising in there. I recall a Spice Girls cover band comprised of five Indian women who looked nothing like the originals other than their costumes.

There were a lot of other people waiting. Some were outsiders like myself, but some were clearly senior employees of the business. We were all being treated equally badly! I was told a few times that I would be seen soon and they would need to find me quickly, so not to leave the waiting area.

After seven hours, an assistant came down to tell me that the Chairman had now reviewed the work, was happy with it, and didn't need to see me. Even though I had flown in specially for the meeting, I could not take offence. My experience was not a result of deliberate rudeness or lack of consideration. It was the appropriate behaviour in a different culture.

I'm talking to Simon. Whether Simon is a broadcaster or businessman depends on who you speak to and what day it is. He regularly pops up on TV and radio to offer a viewpoint or an informed analysis of the news, and he has run a number of successful businesses. With 30 years spent in China, India, Singapore and numerous other Asian countries, it is no surprise many people know his face as the BBC's "Man in the Far East".

"It's a phrase we hear less now, but till recently it was the defining term. But what is the 'Far East'? East for who? East from where? Far compared to what?"

Simon is a little larger-than-life. He has grey hair and glasses, and his speech is clipped and precise. He is in his late 50s, but the sparkle in his eyes makes it easy to imagine him walking the hallowed academic halls of New College, Oxford, in his youth.

"Everything is east of something. But in this case, we are talking east of Europe, specifically Britain. More specifically England. France and England battled it out over who would have possession of zero degrees longitude and England won, so it's in Greenwich. That is where the world starts from, and whilst it may seem like a small thing, it is defining in how we see the world from the West. Time really does define how we see the world.

'Far' is Asia. 'Middle' is the Arab world – somewhere that a certain kind of English person would once go on holiday. My grandmother used to wear a turban, with a big jewel in the middle. It was the fashion at the time. So from the European viewpoint we decide where 'East' is, and how far 'Far' is.

Meanwhile, China has always seen itself as the centre of the world, the Middle Kingdom, from which everything else emanates.

Both sides think they are the centre of the universe. Both sides believe they represent the most advanced version of humanity!

This may sound like a long time ago, the Age of Empire, but it still sets our frame of reference. The big companies date from back then. They have survived since the days of empire to today. Siemens was in China in the 1830s. Unilever has been in Indonesia as a joint British and Dutch venture since around the same time. Phillips were thrown out of China when the

Revolution happened, but a friend told me about walking into a cobweb-covered room in the Forbidden City, just after they started to open up again. The guide pulled a cord, and behold, the room lit up, from a dusty Phillips lightbulb still hanging from the ceiling.

The biggest thing in Asia right now is the Belt and Road. [The Belt and Road Initiative is a global development strategy being driven by China. It currently involves 152 countries and has a target completion date of 2049. It has been dubbed the Silk Road of the 21st century.] But the West isn't set up to even understand what it is. It's not like anything we would do in the West, it's not structured the same. In the West we would plan it, propose budgets, tender, approve and track it. We would treat it as a project.

But this isn't a project. It's a geopolitical ambition. It's cash, power, ambition, influence all ready to scale up and go global. It's not a single thing. It's a long-term dominance plan."

It is important when interacting on a project or decision-making basis in Asia to also be aware that we ourselves are being evaluated. Our perception of time affects how we view events or make plans. It widens or narrows our perception and appreciation. As Westerners we should try and be less obsessed with the now and a little more aware of the past and the future.

We often assume that important things must happen in a tight timeframe and that the most recent action, decision or insight is the most important one. The fact is, what just happened is more likely to be only a part of the bigger picture.

Putting it into action

When considering time perception, we need to think in terms of micro time and macro time. Micro time refers to the day-to-day, which is reflected in how we differ in our perceptions of punctuality, deadlines and commitments. The macro time context is how we differ in our longer-term perceptions – weeks, months, years and even generations.

Micro Time

1 **Schedule meetings at the start of the day**. They are more likely to start on time and much less likely to be cancelled due to late running. And don't schedule anything important for the time slots immediately after a meeting, especially one that's late in the day. You don't want to be the one running late or having to cancel your meetings.

2 **Don't show annoyance if appointments are running late.** Don't vent your frustrations visibly, either to other people waiting with you or to the unfortunate messenger. Word will inevitably get back to your host. Take a book, tablet, music, snacks with you to pass the time.

3 **Don't leave before a meeting has been definitively cancelled.** If you wander off, it will be assumed you've left for good. If you storm off, the meeting will be cancelled permanently and your relationship and reputation damaged.

④ **Salvage a cancellation by making yourself available.** If you have a meeting cancelled at the last minute, give the host or messenger an understanding response, reiterate how important the meeting is to you, and then offer to stay close (e.g. at the lobby or a coffee shop in the building) in case some availability frees up. Often the host will find a way to still squeeze you in. Be flexible.

Macro Time

① **Be aware of the history of relationships.** Take a step back from the immediate situation and ask yourself: What is the background to the relationships in play? How long have they been in place? How does that impact the dynamic? Ask around to get a deeper perspective.

② **Look ahead.** What outside business influences may occur in the next six months, one year and five years that are affecting the thought process and decisions of the parties and stakeholders involved? What about *personal* influences? What are the major economic, social or political changes in the future that may impact the longer-term success of your decisions, actions or projects?

③ **Zoom out to look at the longer term.** How does what is happening look in a 10-year window? Think about five years from now – and of five years *before* now. Balance the immediate benefits with the longer-term effect a decision or an action might have. Remember that your Asian colleagues, partners and clients are doing this automatically.

9:
Risk and Face

"Maintaining face is
about balancing tolerance
for acceptable risk and the
desire for risk aversion.
Always in favour of aversion.
Face is everything. To be
shamed – to not be able to 'show
your face' – is almost unbearable."
— Max, startup founder, 8 years in Asia

Bob takes another sip of his coffee and we sit in silence as our plates are cleared. Bob is a senior agency figure who has worked around the world, including many years in Russia.

"I was sitting in a big meeting with my team in Moscow on a conference call with our global HQ.

The team at global were buzzing over a new pilot project which was going to be run in a regional Russian city. Very prestigious and ambitious assignment, with a very short timeline. The Russian team was less excited. They spent the entire call pointing out all the difficulties and reasons why the project would not be accomplished.

After the call finished, I quickly got another, a direct call from the global leadership. They wanted to know, why wasn't my team excited about the project?

I went back into the meeting room to find that the team were already happily at work on the project they had seemed so reticent about! I asked the team leader why they had been so negative on the call. She explained it to me patiently.

Russians learn fast not to over-commit to anything. Even if they believe something is possible, their natural instinct is to say no. It comes from a deep-seated cultural insight. Failing to deliver in a country that was largely authoritarian for centuries was considered to be a major issue, often with dire personal consequences. Far better to say 'Can't do' initially and then figure out a way to make it happen. That minimises risk.

This was one of my key 'Aha!' moments."

This approach to life – and especially in business – can be very frustrating for people who are used to a more enthusiastic "can do" attitude.

Westerners are often puzzled by what they perceive as the elevated level of caution they encounter, or feel they encounter, when working with individuals or teams in Asia. The reluctance to take a chance, even when the positive opportunity seems to far outweigh the risk, is baffling. Why miss out on an opportunity to show yourself in a good light, win the approval of your bosses, or have your name on a big win?

The answer is risk – and how much of it people are willing to take.

In the West, in general, we are happy to take more risk. We tend to tolerate a larger amount of uncertainty, and we see the more positive upside of a choice and the potential for success. In Asia, there is generally less appetite for risk and uncertainty. When facing the same choices as a Westerner, Asians are more likely to decline the opportunity. Rather than seeing the chance for glory, they see the potential for humiliation.

Low risk-avoidance cultures (the West) are more open to change. They are more receptive to ideas coming from outside the group and team, and are more welcoming of input from younger people. These cultures will give the feeling of being more open-minded, liberal and receptive (although this may often be just the perception). Overall they will have fewer minor laws, and businesses may have less paperwork than high risk-avoidance cultures.

High risk-avoidance cultures (Asia) prefer the status quo, the known, the proven and the safe. They will often see change as a threat and like to stick to established ways of working. The opinions of the old guard will usually carry much more weight than the thoughts of the young guns. These cultures can appear conservative and close-minded, although as mentioned, appearances can be deceptive, and many of the world's most innovative and dynamic businesses and people are in Asia. They may often have a myriad of complex and confusing rules and regulations, and a seemly unending amount of paperwork. More rules and processes, it is believed, will further minimise risk.

Hawker centres are the reason it took a long time for the big fast food chains to get a foothold in Asia. If you want fast, good-quality, tasty and inexpensive food, you go to the hawker centre. McDonald's, KFC or Pizza Hut are neither faster, tastier nor cheaper.

The fast food chains that have succeeded in Asia have recognised this. They offer something different – something premium, exciting and aspirational above and beyond the food. They have realised that whilst the brand may have strong appeal around the world, the positioning needs to be adjusted for the particular context.

In India, McDonald's is a very popular venue for dining in, but delivery and drive-through do not exist. Why? In an economy where a lot of people are still living on dollars a day, McDonald's dining can be a display of spending power. You want to be seen eating there. So the McDonald's in India have large outward-facing windows, and these tables are always occupied.

In Indonesia, KFC is a destination venue. People go to meet friends, listen to DJs and watch live music. The food and drink are the functional elements, but the appeal is much more layered than that. In a country where the majority of people are Muslims, for whom alcohol is not an option, KFC plays the role for young people that pubs and bars play in the West.

I'm sitting in a hawker centre with Joanna. Some 30 or 40 food stalls ring a central dining area. People carrying plates of steaming rice, crabs and satay sticks pass by our table, while young men move from table to table selling coconuts and freshly squeezed sugarcane juice.

Despite having spent nearly 20 years in Asia, Joanna still has a slight Southern US burr. Previously, Joanna held a senior position with one of the world's biggest consumer goods companies; now she heads up the China operations for a global branding and design agency. She is calm and friendly, with long dark hair pulled back into a ponytail.

"When I first came to China, I was given control of a project that was already running through the pipeline. The team was already in place. It was a big, high-profile NPD [New Product Development] piece for a global brand and I just needed to land it.

Unknown to me and the leadership team, there had been a minor screw-up already. The paperwork had been submitted wrongly for the product registration with the government. It would have taken a bit of effort and hassle to rectify, but nothing that couldn't have been fixed, and we would still hit the launch deadline.

About half the team knew about it but decided to stay quiet. They knew that the incorrect submission was working its way through the government process and would be rejected, but they carried on regardless, as though everything was fine. The attitude seemed to be, 'We messed up, but if we keep quiet they won't know who to blame and they can't fire us all.' Rather than admit to a small, rectifiable problem early, with a bit of trouble, they pushed it away and turned it into a huge, negative impact later!

As a result, we missed the launch date on a seasonal product and lost a year of potential sales.

When the company tried to find out what had happened – not to assign blame, but to put in measures to stop it happening again – everyone clouded over the facts, everyone avoided responsibility. We couldn't find out how it had gone wrong, so we couldn't learn from it.

It impacted beyond that project. Globally all projects usually had a post-launch review session, a half-day where the positives and negatives, successes and failures of the project *were openly shared to build best practice and understand where improvements could be made.*

In China that didn't work. Nobody would speak. Nothing positive. Nothing negative. Nothing. Nobody was prepared to lose face by being the one that had any responsibility for any problems. We had to stop implementing part of a globally adhered process because it was pointless.

The result? We didn't adapt the process to suit the local sensibilities, so the process didn't work. We didn't learn from failures, which meant that we were doomed to repeat them. A multi-billion-dollar global company was significantly handicapping its own growth in one of its key markets because it was unable to adapt to the different perspectives of its employees."

Face is not just the tangible manifestation of risk aversion; face is the thing that is actually at risk. Making a choice to speak up, saying yes or no to a deal, making a commitment, having your name on a project – these are all potential ways to lose face. To be attached to a mistake, a failure or a shameful outcome is to bring shame upon yourself, your business and your family.

Risk aversion is a hugely powerful influence in Asia. It can often stop projects that have a small risk of failure from starting or proceeding, or cause projects to move at a snail's pace, as every incremental move forward is validated, assured, double-checked and signed off.

What can be confusing to Westerners is when it appears that the risk avoidance is clearly heading people toward greater risk – when the desire to protect face today will likely result in much greater loss of face tomorrow.

Perhaps the simplest way to think about it is that in Asia, the size of the potential failure is often not as important as your proximity to the failure if it happens. Better a big problem occur that you are not connected directly to than to be associated with a small one.

A powerful example of this is the embarrassment caused during the Singapore Airlines website relaunch. The relaunch of any major airline's website is a large and complex task. Almost all airline bookings, whether by individuals or by businesses, are now made online, so the potential damage that could be caused to the Singapore Airlines brand if the project hit major bumps, or failed to deliver, was huge.

A senior agency lead gave me a summary of what they saw happening. As in every project, there were some problems along the way, but to ensure problems were effectively flagged up, discussed and dealt with, the agency leading the project and building the site had a traffic-light system. Each project task and deliverable was flagged either green, amber or red, and each project stream would be evaluated at the regular catch-up meetings with the agency and client teams. If an orange or a red was flagged up, then the right due diligence would be put in place, the problems addressed and the correct focus and resources attached to solve them.

At one point, with a lot of critical stages occurring, the red flags were appearing more often than some people felt comfortable with. "Stop raising red flags," the senior member of the client team said to the agency before one of the meetings. "All these red flags are making me look bad in front of my boss. From now on, no more red flags." The agency team protested, but the client overruled them.

So no more red flags were raised, the project moved forward, and difficult conversations were avoided. Unfortunately, it meant that problems were buried and patchwork solutions covered up significant issues which needed senior attention. But as requested, no red flags were raised. The client was happy.

But when the site eventually launched, the problems became apparent. Functionality was poor, options previously available had disappeared, the site was slow, it froze, it crashed.

Travellers booking online quickly discovered that if you selected a business class return ticket from Singapore to London, the site only charged you for economy. That glitch cost the airline $1 million (I am told) before they were able to block it.

Angry customers created a petition to bring back the old site. Tech journalists called the relaunch a "botch job". The CEO was forced to make a public apology. For a brand that has built its reputation – even its identity – on delivering high-quality customer service, this was a PR disaster.

So a number of huge problems had occurred because of a reticence to be associated with some small problems. The fear of losing face in the now had blinded people to the bigger problems it was causing.

Why, you may ask, would someone do that? The answer lies in the desire to not stand out, to try and stick invisibly inside the herd, and not draw attention to oneself, in order to avoid the risk of losing face. This powerful desire gives people blinkers to the much bigger, longer-term risks they may be taking.

Max is the fire-juggling startup founder we met in the chapter on Family. With his depth of personal and professional interactions in Asia, Max has a lot of experience observing and negotiating the balancing act of maintaining face.

"You can lose face indirectly. Trust is established by connections and recommendations. You can be passed up the ladder if you build relationships and deliver on what you say. But if you are passed upwards and then do not deliver, that reflects badly on you – as well as on your original connection. So people are very cautious about giving recommendations or testimonials."

Max heads a small but diverse team made up of people from a number of different ethnic and cultural backgrounds. He has learnt to balance Asian caution with the more "gung ho" Western approach.

"There is a culture of 'get your arse out of the firing line' for as long as possible. Then, if action or a decision has to be taken, and no one else has done it yet, just do it at the last minute. This way, if it goes wrong, you can always blame the tight turnaround time!

We once had a Malaysian client that we had a great relationship with. He and his team were happy with the products. The numbers all added up. But the negotiations stalled. The next stage should have been him taking it to his bosses for final sign-off. But it never happened.

We went back over and over again, for more than a year. We relooked the costs. The timelines. The deliverables. He was happy with all of it. Eventually we discovered that although he was 100% happy with our expertise and competence, he wasn't confident in his own understanding of the tech behind the product. He was worried that when he presented it to his bosses, they might ask a question he couldn't answer. That would be bad. He would lose face.

Once we understood the real problem, and realised it didn't lie with us, it was easy to overcome. We offered to accompany him to the meeting with his boss and answer any questions he wasn't sure of. That immediately broke the impasse."

This mismatch of concerns is more common than you would think. Westerners spend a lot of time and effort futilely trying to overcome problems that aren't there, because the real problems are invisible to us.

I found myself in a similar situation on a project in China, where a lot of time and focus was spent battling non-existent arguments. This was a large branding and design project for a dairy company. We had delivered the work, and the work had been used and launched on packs and in campaigns. I had actually seen the products in the supermarket. But we couldn't get the client to pay.

Their rationale was this: Their Chairman hadn't actually liked any of the work, so even though they had used it, they weren't prepared to pay for it. My team and I just didn't understand. We had 100 pages of the strategy and design work, the feedback, the deliverables, the tweaking and rebriefing. No matter how clear we were that work delivered needed to be paid for, we couldn't get past the fact that the Chairman's opinion trumped everything. It was against the contract, against best practice and probably against the law.

Eventually, a Chinese member of our own team told us where we were going wrong. It didn't matter what argument we made about the money. The money wasn't the key issue, it was face.

The guy I was in negotiation with had led the project through to a successful completion, but right at the end, when it was too late to make any changes, he had learnt that the Chairman didn't like the work. Delivering the project on time, coming in under budget, or even the very visible results of the relaunch – none of these were as important as the Chairman's opinion. Bearing in mind the Chairman's displeasure, he needed to find some way of saving face for himself and the team.

The simplest way for him to save face was to pass the responsibility on to the agency, and the way to clearly demonstrate that we were to blame was to punish us by not paying for it.

So we needed to find a way that we would take the blame, and be "punished", but not actually be worse off. I suggested that because the Chairman hadn't been happy, they only pay 75% of the project fee. And for the next project, they would pay only 25% of the usual price. So in effect they would get two projects for the price of one, which meant they weren't really paying for the "failed" project at all.

He readily agreed to that and they actually paid a few days later. He was able to tell people they were getting a project for "free", but we still got paid for (most of) the work delivered. The client and I both knew, really, that there was never going to be another project.

Identifying a win-win solution may thus often involve going against our preconceptions of what a win is. The other party may have a very different idea of what a win looks like. In this case, it was about regaining face from a perceived defeat. Face – not the transaction value – was the valuable element.

Putting it into action

1 **Let yourself see the downside.** In the West, we value positivity, even unrealistic, unwarranted positivity. Allow yourself to see the downsides, the risks and the potential negative consequences of an opportunity or interaction.

2 **Accept that sometimes the glass really is half empty.** Resist the urge to counter Asian colleagues' or partners' caution and reticence with gung ho positivity and the "bright side". You do not need to balance a discussion out. Particularly if the more pessimistic view is actually correct.

3 **Don't project your fears onto others.** They do not necessarily share them. You may fear being seen as too cautious, not ambitious enough, not having enough grit and determination. Others may fear being seen as too risky, too self-serving, too blindly dogged. Avoiding what we fear steers our actions. We do not fear the same things.

4 **Make time and space for the concerns and fears of the team to be aired and acknowledged.** Allow the risks to get put on the table. Don't ignore or railroad over fears. They are valid, and considering them can help you avoid pitfalls and build

a stronger solution. Ignoring them leaves you wide open to charges of "I told you so".

5 **Recognise the seriousness of losing face.** In Asia, the real risk inherent in any venture is not what we think. As a Westerner, we may see the primary risk as the project or task outcome. Did it go well? Did we win? Is the outcome faster, better, cheaper? To many Asians, however, the risk is not the tangible result but the longer-term intangible effect of the result. The shame. The damage to reputation. The loss of credibility. As a Westerner, post failure, we are likely to pick ourselves up, dust ourselves off and crack on with the next challenge. In Asia, the loss of face can be devastating and take years to recover from. When an Asian colleague is displaying what seems to you like undue caution, remember, they have a lot more to lose than you do.

6 **Acknowledge failure and help people move on.** Things will go wrong, projects will derail and sometimes we won't get the outcome we or the team want. It happens. It is tempting to sweep it under the carpet and move on. Don't. Without highlighting any individual failings, take the opportunity to talk about what worked really well, how the team benefited from it, and how it is ultimately invaluable learning, experience and contact-building for the future. This allows people to balance some of the failure with some success. It alleviates self-recrimination and the perceived loss of face.

7 **Don't take a lukewarm response as a sign of disinterest.** It may be masking genuine enthusiasm. In much of Asia, it is

considered safer to be pessimistic than confident. If you raise concerns and reservations, highlight the difficulties, express doubt that something can be done, and then things go wrong, it shows you were right. If on the other hand the project is a success, then it shows that you managed to succeed against all the odds. There is little risk to pessimism, which is why it becomes the default public projection. Take the time to find out people's true sentiments, rather than accepting their projection at face value.

10: Seeing Context

"We think we are the ones playing a game of chess, strategising and making the moves. But we are not. In Asia, we are really part of a bigger game that we aren't even aware of, and we are just the pawns in it."
— Tyson, 20-year Asia veteran in software and telecommunications

In the West, we tend to believe that the environment is influenced by the actions of individuals, that we create the world around us. In Asia, the more widely accepted view is that the individual is formed by the influence of the environment, that the environment creates us.

In the West, we pay close attention to what we and other specific individuals are doing. In Asia, much more attention is given to the bigger picture, the hundreds of influences and variables impinging on a situation.

Cultures that place power, responsibility and choices on the individual are said to have a high internal locus of control.

They believe in getting things done, that the prime driver in life is the individual, and that each of us can make an impact on the world.

On the other hand, people in cultures with a high external locus of control think the opposite. They believe in *being,* not just *doing.* They allow themselves to move in time with the environment, to go with the flow. These cultures may believe more in luck and adhere to superstitions. They tend to be more patient, allowing time to pass and watching things unfold without taking action. They may also feel that many decisions are out of their control, that external forces are the bigger drivers in their life.

This is a subject close to Tyson's heart. Tyson and I are at a hipster coffee bar in Geylang, one of the more edgy parts of Singapore. We are given a choice of coffee beans to choose from, each with its own introduction and tasting notes, like fine wine. We settle by the window, looking out across a carpark to a busy road.

Tyson is highly animated. His voice bounces off the bare concrete walls, and I can't help but think that everyone can hear every word. Given the topic, and that we are the only Caucasians in the place, this makes me slightly uneasy.

"Accepting the nature of how things are is key. You need to appreciate that most people here don't believe they can make much of a change. They believe that they should adapt to the world, that the world doesn't adapt to them.

In the West, we value people who get things done. People who change things. In Asia, that's a mistake. Much better to never have to change things. If it needs changing, it means something was wrong in the first place. People don't like it when you say things are wrong. Better to accept the world as it is.

When I lived in Beijing around the time of the Olympics, it was generally perceived by the authorities that Western-ers could be a source of problems and complexity. The more Westerners in a city, the higher the likelihood that issues that needed to be fixed would arise, the more dents in the order of the world.

One day, we got a knock on the door from the police. They had a list of all the Westerners. They wanted to know our local names – the Chinese nicknames that friends or col-leagues had given us. We gave them, and the Western name on the list was promptly crossed out and a new Chinese name put in its place. One less Westerner living in the city. Fewer Westerners, fewer problems. Less reason to worry. Less need to try and exert control on the world.

The reality had not changed but the perception had. The problem had disappeared. They didn't try to change the real-ity. They changed their perception to match the reality that was in place."

Research has shown that Asians are more likely to adjust their sense of self in the face of changing external dynamics than Westerners. Asians generally agree with the proposition that they are likely to feel differently about themselves depending on the situation, whilst Americans believe that how they feel about themselves is largely independent of external factors.

Asians are also more likely to consciously change them-selves to match their environment and less likely to believe that people have innate differences in their abilities (as found by D.L. Tobin in his study, "The Hierarchical Factor Structure of the Coping Strategies Inventory"). Americans feel that they change the environment to match themselves and believe that what people achieve is due to the differences in their inherent abilities.

How much of an individual's actions is due to who they are, and how much to the context they are in? In "Culture and the Development of Everyday Social Explanation", psychologist Joan G. Miller of the University of Chicago investigated the relative importance of an individual's disposition versus their context in Americans and Indians.

Subjects were asked to talk about their friends, colleagues or neighbours, and to describe times that they had behaved well (positive behaviours) and when they had behaved badly (deviant behaviours). Deviant behaviours might include actions such as taking unfair credit for someone else's work, avoiding taxes or using business funds for personal use.

When asked why they felt the person had behaved in that way, the Americans tended to put the responsibility firmly on the individual – "It's the kind of person they are", "They have always been jealous", "They are very self-absorbed" – whereas the Indians put greater attribution on the role of outside factors – "She isn't working", "He lives far away from school", "It was early in the morning".

Understanding how Westerners value specific actions, reactions and direct effects, whilst Asians are more concerned with the holistic picture, the longer term and the interactions between disparate or associative factors, is key to appreciating why Westerners focus on the actions, whilst Asians understand context.

To put it simply, whilst Westerners are focusing purely on the actor, Asians are paying attention to the whole stage.

Richard E. Nisbett and Yuri Miyamoto make a compelling case for the theory of culturally driven perception in their paper, "The Influence of Culture: Holistic vs. Analytic Perception". When Americans and Japanese were shown multiple farm scenes, each with slight differences, the Americans mostly spotted the differences relating to the main objects in the picture. The Japanese spotted the changes to the background scenery.

When they showed Americans and Japanese a short video clip of fish in a tank, the Americans immediately talked about the bright, rapidly moving fish, whilst the Japanese spent 60% more time talking about the tank.

When they showed Chinese and Americans a picture of a tiger in the jungle, eye-tracking showed that the Americans spent most of the time looking at the tiger, while the Chinese looked around at the whole scene equally – the jungle as much as the tiger.

Yes, the tiger is important, and we should keep an eye on it, but a lot of other dangers – and opportunities – lurk behind and around it, in the rest of the jungle. While fixing our attention solely on the tiger, we may be unaware of the threat from the snake, the crocodile, the tarantula, all lurking in the bushes and trees, as well as the tasty delicacies hidden slightly from view. We should keep an eye out for these things too, but as Westerners, we often don't.

Nisbett and Miyamoto believe these differences are culturally driven. The society in which we are born fundamentally impacts how we perceive things, how we categorise the world, and how we store information in our memories.

As Asian societies are more interdependent than Western ones, perceiving the subtle changes and dynamics of the multiple interdependencies around you is very important. To be happy, successful and popular, you must be deeply attuned to the most insignificant of ripples within the group, the team, the family and the company. You must be able to instantly see and weigh up the big picture.

Mark is a scientist by background, training and disposition. Whenever something takes his interest, he likes to break it down, fully understand how it works, reassemble it and then achieve mastery of it. He runs marathons in a very respectable time, has a black belt in judo, and is a ship skipper. What will tell you most about Mark's character and motivations is that I was friends with him for several years before I learned these facts. Many people (myself included) would manage to drop one of those into the first meeting.

"For me, working my first regional role was frustrating. In Asia, you need to use indirect influence, gaining the trust and respect of others, to have them follow you. But as a Westerner working in Asia, these methods are not apparent. I was trying to take control. I was trying to hard-sell to internal China sales and marketing teams. So for the first couple of years, even though I got airtime at the right meetings, I didn't get any traction at all. I wasn't able to see my role and what I was trying to achieve in the wider context."

Mark and I are at the beach. We are sitting on a log, where the sand meets the grass scrub. His two boys are playing near the water's edge and there is a fresh breeze kicking up the surf.

Mark is in his mid-40s and is lean and fit, with short greying hair. He has a long, expressive face, and his eyes widen when he is engaged in a point. He talks clearly, with a deep and considered intelligence.

"China was already growing and the teams there were doing what they were comfortable and successful with. They didn't really want some foreigner making things complicated for them.

So I switched my presentation around. I looked at what was working and what wasn't, without sidestepping my failure to deliver the HQ's expected growth. Rather than just focusing on what I wanted to achieve, the tasks right in front of me, I put it in the wider context of HQ's expectations for the region.

Afterwards, the China General Manager took me aside, reviewed the "failings" with me, and assigned people to work with me. I then had specific people with the specific directed task of assisting me. Finally I could get things done."

What Mark did, in a very perceptive manner, was to place his needs within the larger business needs. He combined humility and taking personal responsibility with proximity to top-down power. He looked at a specific challenge within the much larger context.

By putting his failures in front of everyone, he opened himself up for help. He was no longer the know-it-all white guy from head office; he was another humble, flawed worker, just like everyone else. He also took personal responsibility, which showed good character. That then opened up the opportunity for the GM to step in.

The West is more culturally individualistic. We put greater emphasis on the individual and attribute credit (and blame!) on the basis of the individual's actions. And the more we look for it, the more we see it, so the more we attribute to it. We would benefit from stepping back a bit, so we can see the wider stage. There are a lot of important things going on in the background that we are missing – things that our Asian bosses, colleagues, direct reports, partners and rivals are very aware of.

I am sitting with Hugo in a cafe in a Southeast Asian luxury mall, overlooking the atrium. Hugo is tall, intense and has an air of easy gravity to him. As we talk, he opens and closes a bottle of sparkling water. He is elegantly dressed in a light-blue blazer and dark slacks, and his hair is pushed back from his long, angular face. Hugo is a C-suite player and an Asia veteran.

"As Westerners we just see what is right in front of us, we don't see the bigger picture. We certainly don't appreciate where we fit in that bigger picture.

I was always good to the staff. If I was given a gift, I shared it. I said hello to everyone, I was polite to all levels of people. Always very professional. But when you're a foreigner, they are watching and talking about you. You can't separate things. There is no work versus personal life, particularly if you are a boss. It is just an unending network of relationships.

I was living in a gated community, with other senior Westerners, other bosses. So I felt insulated. I'd go out, have fun, but always made sure to keep it separate from work. It never affected my work. I was always on time, functioning at 100%.

But it leaks out. You come home late, maybe 4 am. In the morning your driver comes to pick you up to take you to work, maybe 8 am, and as he waits he chats to the security guard. 'Hey, your boss got home late last night. He's a real party guy!' The driver takes you to work, he goes up to the admin team to sign off his hours, sort out paperwork. 'The new boss is a bit of a party guy. Out every night, gets home at 4 or 5 am!' Then it's all over the office. Then it's who they think you are. That's your reputation – but no one will tell you that.

Tiny things get spotted, pieced together, repeated, amplified. One day I was being dropped off at the office by my driver. I opened the car door, stepped out, reached into the car to pick up my bag and a parcel, and because my hands were full, I pushed the door closed with my foot. I didn't even register I had done it. But people saw it. They took it as disrespectful. I heard about it later, that this single action gave me a reputation for being arrogant.

Then there was trouble, a lot of things happening, my role under threat from others, and I was called in to see HR. They had a record that I was a party guy, out every night and coming home in the early hours, and assumed that it must have affected my work. They had statements that I was arrogant and disrespectful to the teams. It wasn't true, but there it was, written down. Perception had become reality."

Hugo's story is by no means unique. Seeing oneself as special, as sitting outside of the larger context, has hampered, or even brought down, many a Westerner's career in Asia or within Asian organisations.

In the West, we talk about work-life balance, as though a separation can wholly exist. We have family, we have friends, we have work colleagues – often all in distinct conceptual spaces. We can move between these groups and sometimes they may overlap, but mostly they remain separate. In Asia, the world does not separate into such boxes. It is a single big picture, a larger context to be aware of and constantly navigate.

But having a special place within the wider context is not necessarily always a problem to overcome – it can be an advantage too, says Tyson.

"Remember that you will always be seen as an outsider. No matter how long you are here, you will always be seen as transient. One of my colleagues told me, 'Whatever happens here, one day you will go home.'

But that isn't necessarily a problem – it can often be a gift. The outsider can get things done without fear of longer-term consequences. You do not need to ensure harmonious relationships with every contact that will extend to your kids in school, neighbours, your next job. You can ruffle feathers and get things done today, without worrying about the relationship in 10 years. You can say the stupid thing that needs saying, as no one expects you to know better. Even though you really do.

Plus, you get allies. One colleague told me he was always supporting and helping me because soon I would go back to global HQ – and then I would look out for him from there!"

Putting it into action

1 **Map out your network of connections – and your connections' connections.** Think of Asia as a 24-hours-a-day, 365-days-a-year personal game of "Six Degrees of Kevin

Bacon", except with you at the centre. Draw a spider diagram of your personal and professional connections, and then for each person, add in *their* connections that you know of. If you do not know their names, just put titles. Your diagram, if you are being thorough, will have dozens or hundreds of names and titles on it. This is just one degree of separation. In Asia, you are influenced by at least three degrees. Bring this awareness into your planning and to your discussions. Ask yourself who else is engaged and influencing, or stands to benefit or lose though the initiative, action or project.

2 **Acknowledge the full context.** Your success is contingent on many external factors, including the contributions of other people. Remember to thank beyond the people in the room or on the email chain.

3 **Be sensitive to the meaning of your actions in a foreign context.** As an outsider, a novelty, you are being watched. Your comments and actions are noted and discussed – by those you know and those you do not know. Your unconsidered (or ill-considered) remarks, jokes or actions will be remembered, and they can come back to haunt you later. As a handy rule of thumb, don't do or say anything that you wouldn't want appearing on YouTube, lest they literally get taken "out of context".

4 **Keep track of special treatment.** As an outsider, you may be credited with wider or more important connections than your local colleagues. As such, you may benefit from additional assistance, support or advice compared to others. You may see decisions swing your way that otherwise wouldn't have. This is

not done through generosity of spirit, but on the expectation that these favours will, due to your special position, be reciprocated later. Be aware (and wary) of whose favours you except.

5 **Frame yourself as another cog in the wheel.** Build empathy with local colleagues and partners by playing down your specialness, and instead focus on the similarity of your situations. Your common challenges from the bosses, your shared frustrations with systems and process, even the bad weather. Place yourself in the same context as them and let them see you as a comrade in arms, fighting the same battle as them, for the same team.

6 **Look at the jungle, not just the tiger.** Don't lose sight of the big picture. Your Asian colleagues and partners will constantly be aware of not just the issue at hand, but also the background, the periphery, the history, the hidden opportunities and pitfalls. They will be factoring these things into their thinking, proposals and solutions. Remind yourself to step back and see the wider context whenever possible.

11:
Corruption & Cronyism

"Corruption is a conceptual relationship between economic agents for the misuse of entrusted power or position."
— Professor Antti Talvitie, Aalto University

Each year, Transparency International publishes its Corruption Perceptions Index, in which it ranks countries according to levels of perceived public sector corruption. A total of 180 countries and territories are ranked according to the results of 13 different surveys, which generate an overall score out of 100, where 100 is very clean and 0 is highly corrupt.

The top 40 places are dominated by the West, with the notable exception of Singapore, Hong Kong and Japan. The bottom 40 places are predominantly sub-Saharan Africa and former Soviet Republic countries. Asian countries mainly score around 30-50 marks out of 100 – not the worst in the world, but a long way behind the standards we see, and are used to, in the West.

Empirically speaking, we can say that Asia is more corrupt than some other parts of the world, and this manifests in the large government corruption scandals that occasionally make headlines (but usually don't), down to the bribes, tips and backhanders that oil the wheels of bureaucracy, commerce and day-to-day life.

As Westerners in Asia, we have a choice: Do we take a grand stand against this, or simply accept it as a fact of life?

Tom is an educator and businessman. He came to Asia for the surfing and to teach. He stayed because he fell in love and whilst here become an accidental CEO. His company supplies large pieces of imported equipment to Asian businesses and government departments. Tom is the epitome of the old adage, "Still waters run deep". His understated appearance and manner give no indication of the globetrotting, surfing entrepreneur that lurks underneath.

Tom talks candidly over dinner about when he and his partner first started up their business in an economically emerging Southeast Asian country, representing an established Western company who until then had no presence on the ground in the region.

"The cronyism and corruption isn't right or wrong – that's just what we project onto it. It just is. It is a fact of life. Recent governments have cracked down on it, but that has just shifted it from the front office to the back room. As a Western business, we cannot be part of it, and I know that has cost us contracts and projects, but that is how we need to be.

But the local client teams recognise our position, and measures are in place to get around it. When we first started out, we would work directly with the local client, submitting figures, filing paperwork, etc. A number of times, it was suggested to us that we use a middleman, a broker. But we didn't see the need for one, we could handle it ourselves, so we declined the option. Now we understand.

How it works is we, the vendor, work with the broker. The broker engages with the client and helps us agree the proposed pricing structure that we will officially be working to. We don't necessarily know what that pricing structure is. The deal gets done, the client pays the broker amount A, the broker passes on to us amount C. Somewhere between A and C, amount B is held by the broker, and is distributed back unofficially to those with influence behind the decisions. This way, we can be competitive while staying squeaky clean.

Some large customers may have a network of preferred brokers that they rotate between, so that you don't have too much money moving though a single person.

This is not what we would think of as corruption. It is not shameful, or particularly underhand, it is simply the process. Now, during the initial conversations with the client, I will ask them if they have a suggestion for a broker that could assist us. It's part of playing the game the right way."

This is a key point to pause on. We instinctively have a reaction when we think of unofficial payments being made, or gifts being given, that may affect the outcome of a process or decision. We have been conditioned to see binary distinctions between right and wrong. What we have described here is bribery, corruption, graft – and to us, that is bad.

But let's be clear, this is a viewpoint, not a universal truth.

In many countries, a payment to an official or any empowered individual to help achieve an aim is totally normal, just like
paying an agent's commission or a processing fee. In fact, many
people would argue that some roles pay badly on the expectation that salaries are topped up with unofficial payments.

Some sources estimate that with large-scale projects,
such as construction or the purchase of large pieces of municipal equipment, up to 50% of the overall cost will go to unofficial
payments to those directly involved in or overseeing the project.

For a long time, this has been seen as an additional hand-
icap for countries that are already struggling under the burdens
of foreign debt and an underdeveloped infrastructure, as they
try to make improvements to the lives of people. The opaque
nature that corruption adds to large projects and government
dealings, and the additional costs it generates, is also believed
to make countries less competitive on the world stage, and
much less attractive to Western investment.

These are not small things, and I am not trying to under-
play them, but this is not the form of corruption you will likely
come face to face with on a day-to-day basis. Most of the
corruption you will encounter is low-level, the kind seen by
Stephen, an educator with 20 years' experience in Asia (who
we hear more from in the chapter on Hierarchy).

*"It is different in Asia. The attitude here is that you can buy
anything. In schools in Asia I have seen a lot of teachers wearing gold watches. Gifts from the parents of pupils. Is that an
innocent expression of appreciation? Or to make sure their kids
get a little more attention or to guarantee the right grades get
given? Who knows."*

Our views on bribery probably aren't as clear-cut as we think, either. If you want a table at a fancy restaurant, do you slip the maitre d' a suitable incentive? Is that bribery? When the waitress brings a round of drinks to your table in a bar and you give her an extra couple of dollars, it that an appreciation for a job well done, or a bribe to ensure good service for the rest of the night?

If we need to draw a line in the sand, perhaps it is this one: The millions of dollars of public money that get funnelled into private bank accounts is 100% wrong; the lower-level government official, the contractor or the waiter expecting a bit extra for their time should probably just be seen as a fact of life.

Yes, it is unarguable that corruption keeps the rich and powerful in place, and has been shown by some sources to slow economic growth. Over time, external and internal forces are reducing the levels of corruption within Asian countries, and this is overall a good thing. But the focus of this book is on how to deal with what is, not dwelling on what we think should be.

In his 2016 paper, "Observed Differences in Corruption Between Asia and Africa: The Industrial Organisation of Corruption and its Cure", Antti Talvitie, a professor at Aalto University, presents a non-conforming, highly insightful perspective on the subject.

Talvitie argues that corruption in Asia is a fixed cost. Businesses and individuals expect it and factor it into their transaction calculations. Costs, selling prices, markups and profits are calculated with a bribery and corruption cost factored in. Whilst foreign powers and institutions wring their hands about this, compile matrices and put up red flags, they don't acknowledge that it is a rational and self-governing structure that is working according to basic human nature and established economic practices. There is no "good" or "evil" within it.

Talvitie points out that the East Asian "economic miracle" of the 1980s and '90s occurred in a number of countries with hugely endemic corruption "problems". Perhaps, he argues, this rapid economic growth happened not in spite of, but partly because of, the institutionalised corruption.

The logic is this: A number of the fast-growing Asian economies are to an extent unstable, or perceived as being so, by those inside and outside them. In these countries, corruption is a means of ensuring that what is supposed to happen, happens, with a minimum of holdups and complications.

In a number of situations, corruption is an illegal transaction that takes place alongside the legitimate one. Talvitie states that the bribery and cronyism that occur within a contract negotiation or project allocation are not in opposition to or even separate to it, but are in fact integral to ensuring the project or contract actually takes place in a timely manner, in accordance with the wishes of those involved.

The holdups, complications and unexpected problems that might stall or even derail a wholly legitimate project have to be overcome, by whatever means necessary. People of power and influence have personally accepted bribes, and what they promised would happen has to happen. The illegal shadow agreements are more binding and likely to deliver results than the wholly legitimate contracts and plans in place.

How, though, does someone know that when the bribe is paid, the official will deliver on their side of the deal – and not simply demand another bribe? This comes down to both parties having a tacit understanding of the rules of the game.

Firstly, the holder of the "official" power needs to stick within realistic fixed costs in order for the other party to be able and willing to engage. Participating in the corruption needs to deliver a preferential financial result compared to not doing so. Simply put, the bribe has to deliver value.

Secondly, the holder of power needs to deliver on their end in order to retain credibility. If they regularly fail to deliver, backtrack or renegotiate, they are no longer a reliable partner, so will not be engaged again. Given the nature of relationships in Asia, an individual's credibility is widely known.

Finally, the credibility and reliability of an individual power holder reflects on all of those holding similar power. If a policeman regularly stops drivers for speeding, takes a bribe and then gives a ticket anyway, pretty quickly word gets round, and soon no one is bothering with the bribe and just opting for the fine. In this case the system is self-regulating – the other officials make it clear that the behaviour is damaging to them and unacceptable.

In Asia, compared to other parts of the world, the depth and length of relationships make corruption viable, less risky and more productive for all involved. This is what makes it a fixed cost.

In other regions, Africa for instance, corruption is a variable cost. You do not know for sure that both parties will hold up their end of the deal, whether they will demand more payments, or whether they can even deliver what they are promising. As a result, corruption rather than "oiling the wheels" is a dangerous variable, which cannot be predicted or relied upon. In these countries, corruption is a clear blocker to growth and advancement – for individuals, businesses and the country overall.

Professor Talvitie outlines the key reasons why corruption persists, despite public discontent and governmental pledges to reduce it.

Firstly, the leader sets the tone, whether it's the CEO of an organisation or the President of a country. The rank and file look to them to see how to behave. If the leadership is corrupt, then others will be too.

Secondly, an individual official who decides not to be corrupt would not change the overall system; they would simply lose out on the benefits of the corruption, and potentially alienate themselves from their peers.

Third, the economic reality is such that many lower-level officials simply cannot afford not to be corrupt. Their salaries are so low that the income from corruption is what allows them to survive. The expectation of corruption income is probably a factor in the setting of these salary levels and the individuals accepting the roles.

Fourth, the bribe-giver is an active participant here too. Without them, there is no corruption. Why pay it? Because if you don't, someone else will. If your business does not pay the bribe to support your project application, your rival, who likely has no such compunction, will be awarded the job. You can't afford not to participate.

Finally, because for a long time the system has worked – at least it has worked for the rich and powerful who control the system – so why fix what isn't broken?

I recall flying into Indonesia for a business trip and getting caught up in the semi-legitimised corruption process. At that point, every trip to Indonesia required a visa on arrival to be purchased at the airport. Each of these took up a full passport page. Flying into Jakarta that day, I realised I was running out of empty pages in my passport. Foolishly I decided to try and peel off some of the previous visa stickers. The first one I tried to remove tore, leaving half on the page and half stuck to my hand. Pulling harder would have ripped out the whole page.

After landing and queuing up, I reached the visa counter window, where the official quickly spotted the torn sticker. He asked me what had happened and whether I knew it was wrong to do it, that it was a serious offence. This was my prompt to offer a bribe, an apology fee, an on-the-spot fine. But I ignored it. I was at the front of a long queue of people and figured the guy surely wouldn't blatantly hustle me in front of so many witnesses. I wouldn't play the game. So he escalated the problem.

I was whisked into a back office, more people started to appear, and the severity of what I had done grew with every new official present. They began to appear to be genuinely offended and angry at what I had done to their visa sticker.

Eventually I took the hint and asked if there was any kind of fine I could pay, to demonstrate my acknowledgment of my wrongdoing and to make amends. The head guy conceded that this could be an option, but it was very serious and I would be facing a large fine. I took all the cash I had and laid it carefully out on the table in front of me. It was the equivalent of about $30.

The assembled officials conferred, and weighed up the various factors that would be used to calculate the amount of my fine. The nature of the offence (severe!), the length of my intended stay in Indonesia (one day), even my profession (which they understood to be advertising) were all factored in. After much discussion, the final amount was calculated and agreed upon by those present. By an incredible coincidence, it happened to be the exact same amount as what I had put on the table.

The money was pocketed, and I assured them I had learnt my lesson. At which point, the whole mood in the room suddenly changed, and we were all buddies. Where was I going for dinner? What did I think of Jakarta? Did I want them to help get me a cab? The game had been played satisfactorily and now we could get on with our days.

A topic related to corruption that always receives a lot of focus when dealing with larger Asian businesses or interacting with government departments is cronyism – the preferential treatment of family, friends, schoolmates, etc.

As Westerners, we tend to work on the assumption that the "best man for the job" should get it. The best offer should win the deal. Hard work and diligence should be rewarded. The idea of people being unfairly rewarded, jumping the queue or landing plum roles simply due to their connections perturbs us.

Western, low-context cultures value transparency and equality. But in high-context, family-orientated cultures such as in Asia, working with friends and relatives is seen as logical and desirable. So while employing relatives is seen as nepotism and frowned upon in the West, it is actively encouraged in Asia.

Hiring or working with a relative, friend, schoolmate or military buddy is seen as having clear benefits in terms of reducing risk. You know their previous work history, you know their credentials are truthful, and there is no need for reference checks. You will likely already know some of their strengths and weaknesses, so there are fewer surprises than if you were to hire a stranger. The relationship also means they are unlikely to suddenly disappear or defect to a rival, taking your trade secrets and client list with them.

This acceptance of the sanctity of family – not just as a support network but as a selection process for career, vendors and partners – extends beyond hiring your relatives to the handing over of power and influence through the generations.

In Asia, it is not uncommon for company boards to be made up almost entirely of family members, even within publicly listed businesses. There is an Indian saying, "Success is a hereditary disease you catch from your parents". Many Indian political figures are second- or third-generation politicians. Most of the current highest-grossing Bollywood actors are the children of the previous generation of Indian movie stars.

A new generation is smoothly handed the reins of economic, political or cultural power by the previous one. This is seen positively by most people in Asia. In a chaotic and unpredictable world, the stability of familial relations provides reassurance.

Perhaps you are still not convinced of the positive aspects of nepotism? How about this – consider the US political stage, which for the last 50 years has been dominated by Kennedys, Clintons and Bushes. Think about the Trudeau family in Canada. Out of the hundreds of millions of people in North America, is it purely coincidence that the best candidates for the highest office just happened to be relatives of previous leaders? Or are there other factors involved?

The British royal family has been "ruling" for over 1,200 years. Nothing lasts that long unless it is giving the public what

it wants – in this case a reassuring sense of continuity and con-
sistency perhaps.

The vast majority of wealth in the West is neither earned
nor grown, but inherited. Warren Buffett refers to the recipients
of these fortunes as the "Lucky Sperm Club". An analysis of the
15 wealthiest multi-generational dynastic families, conducted
by Forbes in 2018, showed that they owned $618 billion. All
of this wealth was built upon companies that their ancestors
founded and built.

So we in the West are not really in a position to look at
Asia and cry "Nepotism!" Yet, we tend to tell a different story.
Business titans like to project an image of "poor boy done good"
when often their background and opportunities gave them a
huge headstart. Billionaires continue to tell a "self-made man"
story, even when their huge inherited wealth is a well-known
fact.

As long as we continue to value the role of the individual above the role of the family in the West, we can't help but
continue to peddle these self-serving, but essentially false, nar-
ratives. In some ways, doesn't this make us less honest, with
our old school ties and family trees, compared to Asia's open
and unapologetic cronyism and nepotism?

Putting it into action

1 **If it helps, think of it as tipping.** Bribery and corruption are
not universal black-and-whites. What you perceive as right or
wrong is specific to your culture and you as an individual, so
do not project your subjective views onto scenarios where that

view is neither relevant nor helpful. See the situation from the viewpoint of the other party, as a perfectly normal request for payment to deliver a service. Not really different from tipping in a restaurant.

2. **Be circumspect about broaching the subject.** Never be the first to mention money. Move step by step through the discussion rather than jumping straight to a bribe. It may not be necessary, or there may be a specific process to work through to keep the bribe semi-official or opaque. Listen and take the lead from the other party. Stay polite and pleasant, but be clear that you have boundaries. Be firm when needed, but do not challenge the other party's authority. Likely it will just lead to an escalation of the discussion with other (more expensive) colleagues

3. **Find out about local practices.** Do not assume all countries in Asia are the same. I cannot stress this enough. Handing a few notes to a traffic cop in Malaysia who has pulled you over will likely result in a smile and you moving along with your day. If you then drive across the Causeway into Singapore and try the same thing, the response will be wholly different, and you will find yourself in the back of their car very quickly.

4. **Engage a middleman.** Is it wrong? Perhaps. But that's the reality. The use of a middleman or broker, particularly if suggested by a client or partner, is a legitimate means of doing business in most of Asia. It ensures that the established means of procuring and conducting businesses can continue, whilst keeping you at arm's length from it.

⑤ **View it as a fixed cost.** Whether you're working out the likely cut going to the middleman, building a complex profit-and-loss model for your business or just how much it's going to cost to get your visa renewed, be realistic about the costs. A business model that makes profit in theory could quickly go bankrupt under the weight of unplanned or unacknowledged costs. Build the fixed, unofficial costs into your business and personal financial expectations. Ignoring it won't make it go away; it will just make you poorer than you expected.

⑥ **Don't forget that cronyism is Western too.** It happens every-where, from small favours to the highest political appointments. In the West we condemn it whilst deluding ourselves about its ubiquitous presence. Asia is open, honest and appreciative of it. If there is any hypocrisy in place, it is with the West. We need to get over it.

⑦ **Remember that there is a line that shouldn't be crossed.** This chapter has focused on the day-to-day business and per-sonal realities for most people. When bribery or corruption begin to compromise or endanger people physically, psycho-logically or sexually, that is time to draw the line. Get away from those situations and people as quickly, and safely, as possible. If you are feeling genuinely threatened, speak to your country's consulate or embassy.

Fieldwork

Fieldwork at Home

You do not need to be based in Asia or within an Asia-orientated culture to start improving your understanding and building the right habits and behaviours.

You could be based in the West and know you will soon be visiting Asia. You could be engaging virtually with an Asian team, or with Western colleagues in Asia. Your company could be looking at acquiring, or being acquired by, an Asian local or multinational player. Or you may simply recognise that Asia will play a growing role in your life in the near future. Whether you go there, or it comes to you, you want to be ready.

You can start to acquire skills and begin to discard your biases with a little effort and without getting on a plane (yet).

Neuroscience research has shown that in the brain, "what fires together, wires together". Repeated actions become habits, and practising a new way of thinking eventually becomes your actual way of thinking. It is possible to change your default settings and knee-jerk reactions permanently, ahead of the time when those behaviours and ways of thinking will actually be regularly required.

This means that the actions you take and the activities you participate in now can prime your brain for success in your future engagements with Asia and Asian culture, whilst you are still at home in the West. Simply put, you don't need to be in Asia to prepare for when you will be.

Below are some of the ways you can do this in a simple, day-to-day manner. They will give you a wider worldview, a larger set of tools, and a valuable cross-cultural perspective.

Movies

If you are a movie buff, make sure you watch the big Asian blockbusters. You will find the action, adventure and romance familiar, but watch out for the nuances. The references to history and culture, the dominance of family relations, the deference to elders. Seek out the critically acclaimed smaller movies, those that go deep into the lives of individuals. There you will find the layers of interconnectedness, the ambiguity, the strive for harmony. The big questions – seen from another perspective.

Some starting points could be:

- "The Way Home" is a Korean movie about a young boy and his grandmother.
- "Shower" is a Chinese comedy revolving around a family-run bathhouse in Beijing.
- "Bride and Prejudice" is a Bollywood take on the classic Jane Austen novel.
- "Leviathan" is a grand social satire on contemporary Russian society.
- "Jiro Dreams of Sushi" is a documentary about a legendary sushi chef in Japan and his relationship with his son.

If you are in a big city, there may be cinemas that cater to the tastes of various cultures. Seeing these blockbusters in a crowd of people cheering along with their favourite action stars, or weeping as their favourite heroine falls foul of a moustachioed villain, is a fantastic learning experience as well as really good fun.

Food

This sounds obvious, but go out and eat other cuisines. Not the Westernised versions, but as near authentic as you can. Don't pick what you recognise. Ask the waiter what he personally likes. If the next table are eating something that looks interesting, ask them what it is. They will be very happy to tell you.

Shopping

A medium to large city will have specialist shops catering to various cultures. They likely won't be big Western-style supermarkets and they will probably be difficult to find. They will be small, crowded, and full of things that are new to you. The staff may seem rude (they may not speak your language), and there may be an unfamiliar smell. But there will also be rows and rows of brands you have never seen, types of fruits and vegetables you don't recognise, products that you have no idea what they are for.... This is a taste of the other side of the world – on your doorstep. Don't miss it.

Books

Browse the international fiction bestseller charts. Don't worry about the author for now. Find a book with a story that you find interesting. If it is not already in English, find the translated version (there is usually a link) and buy an electronic copy so you can dip in and out of it.

If it is a little tough-going, give yourself some breaks and don't try to read too much in one sitting, but do your best to immerse yourself and pay attention to how the scenes differ from what you expect. Are the characters making choices that seem odd to you? Are the traditions and rules they are following strange? These are the rich details to absorb.

News

The fragmented media landscape and the increasingly sophisticated targeting of social media information means it is now possible to remain immersed in information and opinions that reinforce our own pre-existing views.

Confirmation bias draws us to information sources that align with our own. This is perfectly natural as we want to surround ourselves with like minds and those we feel similar to.

But it can also be dangerous. By cutting off most of the information available, we prevent ourselves from experiencing new things and seeing varying perspectives.

This is unfortunate when it happens within our own country and culture – and we are slowly waking up to it. But there is in fact a whole multitude of different views, information sources and opinions coming from outside our "home".

You likely know that BBC, CNN, ABC and Fox have differing views on topics, but what is the view coming from Al Jazeera, CNA (Channel NewsAsia), CGTN (China Global Television Network), GNTV Philippines or Russia-1?

If you read the *New York Times*, try Singapore's *Straits Times* or the *Times of India* instead for a few days. The world's largest-circulation newspaper is *Yomiuri Shimbun* in Japan. In China, *Reference News* is the biggest seller. Step outside of the echo chamber and breathe some fresh air.

Take things a step further by changing your browser settings to a different country. With a few simple clicks, your news feed, advertising, notifications and updates will immediately change. Your computer will become a window to a different world, with products, news, celebrity gossip and human interest stories from the other side of the globe streaming onto your screen.

See how long you can leave it that way!

Sport

Whatever your preferred sport, no matter how mainstream or obscure, most countries around the world will now have at least a national team and often local teams, or talented individuals, playing or participating in it.

You can find the games streaming online or in the high numbers of your cable provider. Seeing your favourite sport being played in front of a wholly foreign but equally passionate crowd is a reminder of our fundamental similarities, as well as the differences.

You can watch the big global sports (soccer, rugby, cricket), or, more interestingly, seek out the sports that are popular in the country of interest to you. Badminton in Indonesia, table tennis in China, baseball in the Philippines. How other countries have embraced these sports and made them their own is fascinating.

To really see things from a new angle, watch a large tournament you would watch anyway, but view it on a foreign channel. Watch your home country play an Asian team, and listen to the Asian country's commentary of it.

Be aware of your own biases

When entering new worlds, meeting new people or approaching new situations, we need to recognise that our existing perspectives are just one way of viewing the world.

We should consider our backgrounds, our cultures and our societal norms. Acknowledge that we have preferred reactions and unconscious biases, and that our responses are often neither considered nor objective. They are automatic and highly subjective.

We have one worldview that is uniquely ours; no one else totally shares it. Take time to understand what your views are and how they were formed.

Consider the specific beliefs and habits of your family, your town, your school, your college or university, your religion, your country. Try to think of at least three things for each that are important to that group and not necessarily prioritised as highly by others.

It could be a way of interacting within the group, or with people outside of it, perhaps a communication norm, a way of talking, responding, a greeting, or even an emotional or physical taboo. What are you expected to do? What are you not allowed to do?

Ask yourself, how many of these were you previously aware of as different from the mainstream? Consider which of these habits or views have become ingrained in your behaviours inside that group – and do you follow these rules when working and engaging with people from outside the group?

This is a hugely important shift in thinking. Most people will never recognise that their view is just one of many differing views inside and outside of their own country and culture. They spend their lives assuming everyone thinks the same way and are baffled, and possibly threatened, by any behaviour that differs from their expectations.

If you can move away from this narrow way of thinking, then you already have a clear and actionable advantage over the majority.

But this exercise is just the tip of the iceberg. There are many more behaviours and attitudes specific to you and your groups that you are wholly unaware of. You don't need to stop thinking them, or acting on them; just constantly remind yourself that they are just your way of thinking and acting, not *the* way. Everyone has their own set of behaviours, norms, thought processes, taboos and preferences, every bit as unique as yours. The further you travel, the greater the variety you will see and engage with.

Fieldwork Abroad

It is common when travelling for business to find ourselves in a tight little loop or bubble. Airport to hotel to office to taxi to airport again. It is understandable – you are busy and there is a lot to do. You don't know the city, it seems scary out there, it smells a bit strange, and the people look different.

But it is vital to break the loop. Below are some suggestions on how to get much more from your trips to new countries or your new home.

Take a walk

Get up, put on your shoes, walk to the hotel lobby and go out. HBO and Pringles will still be there when you get back, and you will have a thousand opportunities to lie on a bed in your underwear in the future. But you may never get the chance to explore this particular city again.

If you're a bit wary, start with something very, very achievable. Ask the hotel staff to recommend a local bar, restaurant or park within easy walking distance. They will likely be overly cautious, so they will not send you awry. In fact, they may try to talk you out of leaving the hotel on your own!

Pick a destination 5–10 minutes away and walk there. Keep the hotel location clearly in mind. Keep your eyes and your mind open. If you spot something interesting on the way, by all means stop and investigate it. Don't be too focused on getting to your destination.

Eat out

Don't eat in the hotel, the office cafeteria, or the global food chains near the office. I promise you, you will find something a lot more interesting to eat by walking just five minutes out.

It may not be your comfort food and it may not become your favourite – in fact you may not really enjoy it – but you will certainly learn from it. You will likely remember it more than most of the meals you eat (you eat three meals a day, every day of your life – how many do you remember?).

From simply sitting down in a new environment, surrounded by new people and trying new food, you will get an idea of the place, the people, and the habits of the culture you are in. It will nourish your mind and soul as well as your body.

Ask the locals

Everyone likes to give advice, because we all like to demon-strate our expertise in something.

Asking your team, colleagues, suppliers or clients for advice on where to go and what to do not only builds relation-ships, it gives you suggestions for activities that will actually reflect the interests of the people you work with. It will get you out of the usual tourist traps too.

In Asia, food is the safest topic to use as an ice-breaker or a relationship-builder. In many Asian countries, "Have you eaten?" or "Did you take lunch yet?" are the generic greet-ing questions. They fulfil the function of "How are you?" in the West.

Whilst this question doesn't often require an in-depth answer ("Yes, you?" will suffice), it does give you an opportu-nity to mine for further information.

If a venue is mentioned, or a food type described, return to that topic later. Ask where the venue is – is it near the office or your hotel? Is it open for dinner and lunch? You then have suggestions for where to go, and you have built a stronger con-nection with the contact.

The next step: Politely ask your local contacts, colleagues or clients if perhaps they could take you out. Not to wine and dine you, and not to somewhere they only go because they feel you will be comfortable there. Ask for somewhere they would go with their family or friends.

If you are uncomfortable directly asking to be taken out, ask the local team in conversation about their weekends or eve-nings. Where did they go, what did they eat? If you express interest in going yourself, they may invite you.

This isn't about trying to become best friends with the team, although they will probably appreciate that you are making the effort to get to know them, nor is it about ingratiating yourself. It's about insight and getting an authentic idea of how people live, what they like and how they act when some of the barriers are down.

Extend your stay by half a day

We are all very busy – or like to feel and project that we are – so it is hard to break off some time for ourselves. We need to get back and be seen at the office, or we want to get home to our families and friends.

We often think we can't justify spending half a day exploring a city before or after our set schedule, but in fact we can't justify *not* doing so. The benefits of spending some time out of the office, hotel or airport and really seeing a place are immeasurable.

So get out of the hotel and do something that can only be done in that location. Don't go to an international mall or a global fast food restaurant. Find a local food court, look for someone eating something interesting and ask them which stall it's from. They will be happy to tell you, and will probably escort you over to it and help you order.

Go to the park, watch the families playing and the retirees exercising in their group classes. Sit outside at a bar on a busy street and savour a cold beer. Watch the bustle of a busy city going about its business and strike up a conversation with the next table.

Arts, recreation and sport

With a little planning, you can go and watch a live sports event when you are in the field. Being lost in a foreign crowd all cheering in unison is a truly immersive experience. It gives great insights into the culture and people and is a brilliant means of finding common ground for conversation and affinity with your local colleagues and partners.

Whatever your preferred leisure activity, you can likely do it on your travels or in your new home location.

If you run at home, even if just occasionally, run when you are away. If you don't run at home, you probably should, and this is a great way to start. Pack a pair of running shoes in your luggage. Many hotels have a running club, so sign up and join in. If the hotel has nothing organised, just lace up and go for it. Twenty minutes around the block is good for body and soul and lets you see the neighbourhood.

Don't plug in your earphones, but listen as you run. Earphones isolate you and block out a whole dimension of any experience. The sounds of people, the traffic, the shouts, the laughter, the animals – these are as vital as the sights.

For team sports, look online and search social media. There could be a pick-up game in your local park. You will often see casual softball, soccer or basketball games taking place. In India, Pakistan and Bangladesh, every piece of spare land has a cricket game happening on it. Wander over and see if you can join in.

If you are near the coast, there will be clubs, hire centres and drop-in schools for a range of watersports like surfing, dragon-boating, paddle-boarding and sailing. This is a great way to see the country from a fresh angle, and to build an instant peer group of like-minded enthusiasts.

Museums, art galleries and exhibitions are a window into the local culture and a great way to meet people too. You can look online and see what is available at the local municipal art gallery or museum. There almost always is one. It may have a cultural or historical emphasis, but that's great as it will give you a deeper appreciation of where you are. Works by local artists give you a feeling of the buzz, the mood beneath the surface.

Listen to the local music. Not necessarily the "traditional" forms, but the popular bands and artists. Note the similarities and the differences compared to what you usually listen to. If possible, go to local gigs, big and small. Watch the band, and just as importantly, the crowd.

All of these things are a great way to broaden and deepen your appreciation of the country and culture, but will also give you the building blocks for stronger relationships with the locals you interact with professionally and socially. They provide common experiences, talking points, and most importantly, they demonstrate that you value and appreciate their culture, and that you are willing to put in the effort and the time to find out and experience more. It shows you are building a bridge, which encourages people to start building from their side too.

Shopping

Retailers talk about the "modern" and "traditional" trade. Modern trade stores are the big supermarkets, global chains, and the local brands that emulate the style and scale of the big players. If you get a chance to visit one in a new country, do so. Whilst a lot of it is familiar, you will find rows of brands you have never seen before, whole categories of products you didn't know existed, and ways of selling you couldn't imagine (like the tanks full of live frogs in a Shanghai Walmart!).

To really experience local shopping, leave the chains and visit the traditional trade stores. These are the small mom-and-pop stores, often family-run, with the extended family living above. They either specialise in a very small number of products (just varnish, or only durians), or they stock what appears to be a million things.

And when you feel brave enough, go to the wet market. These are the marketplaces where food is piled high and sold fast. Fruit and vegetables still have dirt on them, meat is still bloody and glistening, and the seafood still wriggles and snaps its claws. These markets tend to open at daybreak and close by lunchtime, so go early.

All this fieldwork – whether at home or abroad – widens your perspective, gets new sparks firing in your brain, and grows you as a person. It will give you an extra connection to the local teams, the senior players, the suppliers and the contacts that your competition (in and outside your organisation) does not have. You will have a rare superpower. You will have local-vision.

Final Words

This book has mainly looked at the challenges faced by individuals and businesses coming to Asia. But the Asia/West convergence is not one-directional.

Paula was an early employee of an online retail startup in Singapore, which grew quickly. It attracted the attention of a large Southeast Asian regional player, which bought the controlling share. Not long after, a giant Chinese retail player, the biggest in the sector, gobbled up control of both. As three different ways of working collided, Paula saw the struggles across all camps as they tried to work together:

"In China, all the company's employees followed the Chairman's lead and had committed to '996'. That meant working from 9 am to 9 pm, six days a week. This was a culture of chants, team celebrations and group displays of allegiance and commitment. In China this worked, as they are the destination employer, everyone wants to work for them, there is a real esteem to being part of it. For every job available, thousands apply for it.

And that is how they saw themselves. It was very hard for them to accept the fact that outside of China, they were just another big company, and even harder to change their behaviours and expectations.

The belief was they would bring over successful senior guys from China, put in place their culture and way of working, and replicate the success in multiple countries. There was very little thought given to adapting to local cultures or leadership styles.

This combination of incredibly high expectations and indirect communication style caused problems immediately. The Chinese managers couldn't understand what was going wrong, as they were doing exactly the same thing that had been so successful in China. Why wasn't it working?

Employee turnover was huge, 50% in some locations. It was a huge stumbling block, and I think it made them question the whole strategy. They are now starting to realise that they cannot expect all markets to follow 'the way' and need to adapt accordingly, that the most successful managers in the home market are not necessarily the best people to work in or lead new markets. Sometimes those who are most successful in a particular system are those who are most unable to (or unwilling to see why they should) shed that way of working and adapt to a new system.

Now the support systems and the back end are all still managed from China, but increasingly the local markets are adapting more to the specific needs and developing their own ways of operating. The second wave of Chinese managers are more open to this and to adapting to the cultures. But learning this was hugely painful, cost millions of dollars and probably stalled growth substantially."

Shedding preconceptions

Andy is a big chap. He has the build of a rugby player. He is a highly successful, multi-award-winning creative director. His name is well-known in the advertising industry, and he knows how to communicate very effectively.

We are having lunch in a small restaurant on a busy street. It is crowded, and without having reservations we have been given a small table at the back of the room. We manoeuvre our phones and wallets around the table to make room for our plates. We both shift around in the seats. Occasionally our feet bump under the table as we try to stretch a little.

"Have I told you about my shirts? Well, I'm big. I'm six feet and four inches. I weigh 115 kg. I'm pretty affable – my old man used to call me his gentle giant – but when people first meet me, they can be intimidated.

I'm very aware of that. So I wear a pink shirt. Why? Because it has a calming effect on people. Which means I can come across as more approachable.

As outsiders, we make a huge impression. We stand out in Asia. Our offhand comments have weight. We make an impact, for better or worse. We need to be aware of this, and think and act accordingly.

We often don't see the baggage we carry. We have so many preconceptions, rigid thoughts, ways of working attached to us. A lot of our views are clutter. But we don't realise we are carrying them around with us.

My old boss once told me a lovely story that went like this. A journalist had heard about an incredible wood-carver who was making a stir in Mumbai. People were flocking to his little shop, situated in the heart of the bazaar, to snap up his lifelike elephant carvings.

Curious, the journalist decided to pay the wood-carver a visit. She stepped through the entrance of his small shop and immediately spied rows of elephant carvings on a long shelf. Each one had a paper tag hanging around its neck with the word 'Sold' written on it. The small and wizened man, with a chisel in one hand and a mallet in the other, was doing good business.

'May I?' said the journalist, as she picked up one of the elephants. The wood-carver gave a little nod and continued working on the next masterpiece in front of him.

'Your elephants are beautiful,' continued the journalist. 'They're so lifelike. They have so much character. They're more elephanty, dare I say, than an elephant. How do you do it?'

At that, the old wood-carver looked up at the journalist and replied, 'I take my little knife and I take a block of wood. Then I carve away everything that is not an elephant.'

The moral of the story? Much of what we do and how we view the world has big chunks of wood attached to it. Wood that needs to be carved away to reveal the elephant beneath. We need to strip away everything that is not needed in our views and see things fresh."

This is great advice. Step back, take a breath and look afresh not just at what's around you, but at yourself.

You talk funny, not them

One common mistake Westerners make is that they forget they are interacting with people who are operating in their second or perhaps third language. They think that a few pauses or a misused word are a reflection of the person's intelligence.

"A person's skill in English is not indicative of their intelligence or understanding. The only thing it is an indicator of is how well they can speak English. Which is usually much better than how well the Westerner can speak their language."

Erica, a Canadian design and education professional, has spent 15 years in Asia, and has seen first-hand the challenges in communicating across a language divide.

"We also often use terms and phrases that don't have any literal relation to what we know they mean. Let the cat out of the bag. Run it up the flagpole. Plenty more fish in the sea. These are incredibly hard to understand and make it very challenging for non-Westerners to communicate with us."

Humour in a different language or from a different culture is also very hard to understand. Jokes work when the punchline is unexpected, or contradicts the set-up. But this is culturally specific. Trying to use jokes to put another person or group at ease, or to make a connection, may not work, as it will likely highlight the differences between your understandings, and may cause awkwardness. Whether it is a team meeting, a big presentation or just trying to be friendly to the server in a coffee shop, better to not try to be funny. Erica's advice:

"Stick to talking about food – that's the great bonding topic in Asia."

Don't forget what you don't know

A little knowledge may be a lot better than none, but we need to remain highly aware of the gaps in our knowledge.

A good friend of mine was presenting to a roomful of marketers in Guangzhou and it was going really well. He had built up a good rapport with them and established himself as a subject matter expert, whilst ensuring they clearly remained the unquestioned experts on their business and customers.

"As we were wrapping up, I made a seemingly offhand comment, which was designed to demonstrate my depth of character as well as my intelligence: 'Let's remember, today is a gift.'

The boss took notice. 'Sorry, what was that?' she asked.

I elaborated: 'Yesterday is history, tomorrow is a mystery, today is the present. That is why it's a gift.'

The room went silent and the boss mulled it over. 'I really like that. Who said it originally?' she asked.

By now I was thoroughly enjoying my new role as sage and wise man. Without much thought I replied, 'I believe it was Confucius.'

From the back of the room, the most junior member of the client team, who until this point had been completely silent, looked up from her laptop and said, in a voice loud enough for everyone to hear, 'Actually, it was Kung Fu Panda.'

I am not sure what went out the door quicker, me or my credibility."

As the woman in this meeting knew, just enough relevant, actionable information, at the right time, makes all the difference.

Acknowledgements

My immense gratitude goes to the thinkers and leaders who generously shared their time and experiences with me: Mark, Penny, Andrew, Simon, Joanna, Navneeta, Max, Tyson, Dane, Ian, Jay, Karsten, Bob, Peter, Zeina, Stephen, Jack, Jen, Ray, Rebecca, Tobias and Tom.

Thanks to Maya, James and Matt for their support.

Thanks to Melvin, Mindy and Justin at Marshall Cavendish, for their help every step of the way and explaining to me how this whole thing works.

Thanks to my Mum and Dad for their utter belief in me and the confidence that gave.

And thank you, Erica, my wife, adviser, partner and best friend, for making absolutely everything in the life we have possible.

For more information, resources and expert interview clips,
visit the **Surfing the Asian Wave** website at
stevenmcginnes.com